THE U.S. ARMY RAPPELLING HANDBOOK

MILITARY ABSEILING OPERATIONS

FULL-SIZE 8.5"X11" CURRENT EDITION

TC 21-24

Headquarters, Department of the Army

The US Army Rappelling Handbook - Military Abseiling Operations

Techniques, Training and Safety Procedures for Rappelling from Towers, Cliffs, Mountains, Helicopters and More - Full-Size 8.5"x11" Current Edition - TC 21-24

U.S. Army

This edition first published 2019 by Carlile Military Library. "Carlile Military Library" and its associated logos and devices are trademarks. Carlile Military Library is an imprint of Carlile Media (a division of Creadyne Developments, Las Vegas, Nevada). The appearance of U.S. Department of Defense (DoD) visual information does not imply or constitute DoD endorsement. New material copyright © 2019 Carlile Media. **All rights reserved.**

For information purposes only.

Published in the United States of America.

ISBN-13: 978-1-949117-11-0
ISBN-10: 1949117111

www.**CARLILE.MEDIA**
THE **ACTION** PUBLISHERS

Training Circular
No. TC 21-24

*TC 21-24

Headquarters
Department of the Army
Washington, DC, 9 January 2008

Rappelling

Contents

		Page
	PREFACE	vi
Chapter 1	**TOWER RAPPELLING**	1-1
	Section I - Personnel	1-1
	Rappel Master	1-1
	Rappel Safety Officer	1-2
	Rappel Lane NCO	1-3
	Rappeller	1-3
	Belayer	1-4
	Belay Safety	1-4
	Section II - Preoperations Briefings and Safety Procedures	1-4
	Safety	1-4
	Safety Briefing	1-4
	Tower Safety and Preparation	1-5
	Rappeller Preparation	1-6
	Section III - Rappelling Procedures	1-7
	Seat-Hip Rappel	1-7
	Australian Rappel	1-13
	Climbing Procedures	1-13
	Tower Procedures	1-14
	Rappel Tower Training for the UH-1H Helicopter	1-16
	Rappel Tower Training for the UH-60 Blackhawk Helicopter	1-17
	Emergency Lock-in Procedures	1-17
	Communications	1-18
	Demonstration	1-18
Chapter 2	**GROUND RAPPELLING**	2-1
	Personnel	2-1
	Sustainment Training	2-1
	Selection of a Rappel Point	2-1
	Establishment of a Rappel Anchor Point	2-2
	Establishing the Rappel Lane	2-4
	Operation of the Rappel Point	2-5
	Recovery of the Rappel Point	2-7
	Types of Rappels	2-7
Chapter 3	**HELLICOPTER RAPPELLING**	3-1
	Section I - Personnel	3-1
	Rappel Master	3-1
	Rappel Safety Officer	3-1
	Pilot-in-Command	3-1
	Rappeller	3-1
	Belayer	3-2

Distribution Restriction: Approved for public release; distribution is unlimited.
*This publication supersedes TC 21-24, 10 September 1997.

Contents

	Page
Section II - Training	3-2
Sustainment Training	3-2
Refresher Training	3-2
Section III - Preoperational Briefings and Safety Procedures	3-2
Medical Coverage	3-2
Communication Requirements	3-2
Adverse Weather/Terrain Conditions	3-3
Night Operation Requirements	3-3
Safety Briefing	3-3
Section IV - Deployment of Ropes	3-4
Deployment Bag Technique	3-4
Log Coil Technique	3-4
Section V - Rappelling Operations for the UH-1H Iroquois Helicopter	3-5
Characteristics	3-5
Rigging the UH-1H Helicopter for Rappelling	3-5
Construction of Anchor Points	3-6
Seating Arrangements and Loading Techniques	3-8
Rappelling Procedures	3-9
Rappelling Commands	3-10
Inspection and Safety Considerations	3-13
Section VI - Rappelling Operations for the UH-60 Blackhawk Helicopter	3-13
Characteristics	3-13
Rigging of the UH-60 for Rappelling	3-13
Seating Arrangements and Loading Techniques	3-15
Rappelling Procedures	3-16
Rappelling Commands	3-17
Inspection and Safety Considerations	3-17
Section VII - Rappelling Operations for the MH-53 Helicopter	3-17
Characteristics	3-17
Rigging of the MH-53 Helicopter for Rappelling	3-18
Seating Arrangements and Loading Techniques	3-18
Rappelling Procedures	3-18
Rappelling Commands	3-18
Inspection and Safety Considerations	3-19
Chapter 4 EQUIPMENT	**4-1**
Section I - Ropes	**4-1**
Types of Ropes	4-1
Rope Selection	4-2
Section II - Snaplinks	**4-3**
Description	4-3
Types of Snaplinks	4-3
Inspection	4-5
Gloves	4-5
Section III - Alternate Methods of Descent	**4-5**
Figure-Eight Descender	4-6
Munter Hitch	4-6
Chapter 5 ROPE MANAGEMENT AND KNOTS	**5-1**
Section I - Preparation, Care and Maintenance, Inspection, Terminology	**5-1**
Preparation	5-1
Care and Maintenance	5-1
Inspection	5-3

	Page
Terminology	5-3

Section II - Coiling, Carrying, Throwing **5-5**
Coiling and Carrying the Rope 5-5
Throwing the Rope 5-8
Section III - Knots **5-8**
Square Knot 5-9
Fisherman's Knot 5-10
Double Fisherman's Knot 5-11
Figure-Eight Bend 5-12
Water Knot 5-13
Bowline 5-14
Round Turn and Two Half Hitches 5-15
Figure-Eight Retrace (Rerouted Figure-Eight) 5-16
Clove Hitch 5-17
Wireman's Knot 5-18
Bowline-on-a-Bight (Two-Loop Bowline) 5-19
Two-Loop Figure-Eight 5-20
Figure-Eight Loop (Figure-Eight-on-a-Bight) 5-21
Prusick Knot 5-22
Three-Loop Bowline 5-23
Transport Knot (Overhand Slip Knot/Mule Knot) 5-24
Kleimheist Knot 5-25
Frost Knot 5-26
Girth Hitch 5-27
Munter Hitch 5-28
Rappell Seat 5-29

Appendix A   **RISK ASSESSMENT** A-1
Appendix B   **BASIC EQUIPMENT FOR RAPPEL OPERATIONS** B-1
                               GLOSSARY Glossary-1
                               REFERENCES References-1
                               INDEX Index-1
                               DA Form 5753-R .... behind Index

Figures

Figure 1-1. Static rappel tower 1-1
Figure 1-2. Example of rappel tower anchor points 1-6
Figure 1-3. Construction of rappel seat .... 1-8 through 1-12
Figure 1-4. Australian rappel 1-13
Figure 1-5. Example of arm-and-hand signal GET READY 1-14
Figure 1-6. Example of arm-and-hand signal POSITION 1-15
Figure 1-7. L-shape position 1-15
Figure 1-8. Example of arm-and-hand signal GO 1-15
Figure 1-9. L-shape position while rappelling 1-16
Figure 1-10. UH-1H helicopter skid rappel training 1-17
Figure 1-11. UH-60 helicopter rappel training 1-17

Figure 2-1. Rope tied to anchor with anchor knot 2-2
Figure 2-2. Self-equalizing anchors 2-3
Figure 2-3. Pre-equalized anchor 2-4
Figure 2-4. Effects of angles on an anchor 2-4
Figure 2-5. Hasty rappel 2-8
Figure 2-6. Body rappel 2-9
Figure 2-7. Seat-hip rappel 2-10

Contents

		Page
Figure 2-8.	Proper hookup using carabiner wrap	2-11
Figure 2-9.	Figure-eight descender	2-12
Figure 2-10.	Extended hookup with self-belay	2-13
Figure 2-11.	Patient secured to carrier's back	2-14
Figure 2-12.	One-man carry	2-15
Figure 3-1.	Coiling log	3-5
Figure 3-2.	Donut ring attached to the floor of the helicopter	3-6
Figure 3-3.	Donut ring and rappel rope connection in a helicopter	3-6
Figure 3-4.	Floating safety ring formed with two snaplinks	3-7
Figure 3-5.	Rappel rope connection using two snaplinks for the floating safety ring	3-8
Figure 3-6.	Four rappel ropes connected to the floating safety ring (two snaplinks)	3-8
Figure 3-7.	UH-1H seating arrangement	3-9
Figure 3-8.	Arm-and-hand signal for GET READY	3-11
Figure 3-9.	Arm-and-hand signal for SIT IN THE DOOR	3-11
Figure 3-10.	Arm-and-hand signal for THROW ROPES	3-11
Figure 3-11.	Primary arm-and-hand signal for POSITION	3-12
Figure 3-12.	Alternate arm-and-hand signal for POSITION	3-12
Figure 3-13.	Arm-and-hand signal for GO	3-13
Figure 3-14.	Primary snaplink attaching point	3-14
Figure 3-15.	Secondary snaplink attaching point	3-14
Figure 3-16.	Primary and secondary snaplink attaching points	3-15
Figure 3-17.	UH-60 rappelling personnel seating arrangement	3-15
Figure 4-1.	Kernmantle rope construction	4-1
Figure 4-2.	Nylon-laid rope	4-2
Figure 4-3.	Standard snaplink (oval)	4-3
Figure 4-4.	D-shaped snaplinks	4-4
Figure 4-5.	Locking snaplink	4-5
Figure 4-6.	Figure-eight descender	4-6
Figure 4-7.	Munter hitch	4-6
Figure 5-1.	Example of completed DA Form 5752-R	5-2
Figure 5-2.	Examples of roping terminology	5-4
Figure 5-3.	Mountain coil	5-5
Figure 5-4.	Butterfly coil	5-6
Figure 5-5.	Butterfly coil tie-off	5-7
Figure 5-6.	Square knot	5-9
Figure 5-7.	Fisherman's knot	5-10
Figure 5-8.	Double fisherman's knot	5-11
Figure 5-9.	Figure-eight bend	5-12
Figure 5-10.	Water knot	5-13
Figure 5-11.	Bowline knot	5-14
Figure 5-12.	Round turn and two half hitches	5-15
Figure 5-13.	Figure-eight retrace (rerouted figure-eight)	5-16
Figure 5-14.	Clove hitch	5-17
Figure 5-15.	Wireman's knot	5-18
Figure 5-16.	Bowline-on-a-bight	5-19
Figure 5-17.	Two-loop figure-eight	5-20
Figure 5-18.	Figure-eight loop (figure-eight-on-a-bight)	5-21
Figure 5-19.	Middle-of-the-rope Prusik knot	5-22

Page

Figure 5-20. End-of-the-rope Prusik knot 5-22
Figure 5-21. Three-loop bowline 5-23
Figure 5-22. Transport knot (overhand slip knot/mule knot) 5-24
Figure 5-23. Kleimhiest knot.. 5-25
Figure 5-24. Frost knot 5-26
Figure 5-25. Girth hitch.. 5-27
Figure 5-26. Munter hitch 5-28
Figure 5-27. Rappel seat... 5-29

Tables

Table 1-1. Rappeller commands 1-18

Table 2-1. Rappel commands 2-5

Table A-1. Risk assessment matrix... A-2

Preface

This training circular provides basic rappelling techniques to Soldiers and leaders for the conduct of rappelling operations. It serves as the primary reference for both resident and nonresident instruction presented to cadets, officer candidates, and commissioned or noncommissioned officers. Guidelines on how to conduct safe rappelling operations are also contained in this training circular. The safety notes and considerations presented provide only minimal acceptable standards. Rappelling is inherently dangerous; so commanders at all levels must analyze the complete training event to determine the degree of risk involved to men and equipment. After determining the risks, risk reduction options or controls should be integrated into the training activity. These options or controls may range from safety briefings—to providing additional safety resources—to selecting other means of accomplishing the mission.

This publication applies to the Active Army, the Army National Guard (ARNG)/Army National Guard of the United States (ARNGUS), and the United States Army Reserve (USAR) unless otherwise stated.

USASOC Regulation 350-2, *Training Airborne Operations*, 27 September 2001, and USSOCOM Regulation 350-6, *Training Special Operations Forces Infiltration/Exfiltration Operations*, 25 August 2004, contain relevant information for rappelling operations but are not readily available.

The proponent for this publication is the U.S. Army Training and Doctrine Command. The preparing agency is the U.S. Army Infantry School.

Unless this publication states otherwise, masculine nouns and pronouns do not refer exclusively to men.

Chapter 1
TOWER RAPPELLING

Introduction to rappelling is taught on a static tower (Figure 1-1). Using the building block approach to training, Soldiers systematically progress to more demanding platforms including taller static towers and helicopters. The static tower used may vary in size and height from 34 to 90 feet. The concept of learning basic rappelling techniques before helicopter operations does not vary.

Figure 1-1. Static rappel tower.

NOTE: Static rappel towers should resemble the structure or aircraft of their training objective. Plans and designs for static rappel towers can be obtained through the DPW (Directorate of Public Works) Engineering Div, Bldg 6, Fort Benning, Georgia 31905 (706 545-1591/DSN 835-1591). Strict adherence to design specifications is required for safety. Rappel towers should be inspected annually by post safety or post engineers. Installations, MACOMs, and unit commanders may establish additional policies and safety procedures as needed to ensure safe and effective rappelling operations.

SECTION I — PERSONNEL

1-1. This section discusses the personnel involved in training rappelling and their duties and responsibilities.

RAPPEL MASTER

1-2. The proponent for accreditation, evaluation, and information for Army rappel master courses is G3, Directorate of Operations and Training, U.S. Army Infantry School, ATTN: ATSH-TDD, Fort Benning, Georgia 31905-5593.

Chapter 1

DUTIES AND RESPONSIBILITIES

1-3. The rappel master is responsible for rappeller safety, the serviceability of all equipment (installation, unit, and personal property), and the personal supervision of rappelling operations.

QUALIFICATION

1-4. Rappel master qualification is awarded only after the successful completion of a TRADOC accredited rappel master course that includes the following subjects:
- Duties and responsibilities of a rappel master.
- Safety SOP, regulations, and references.
- Construction of a deployment bag.
- Conduct of an equipment rappel off the rappel tower.
- Conduct of a lock-in.
- Talking a rappeller through completion of a rappel.
- Conduct of ground training.
- Inspecting for proper hook-ups.
- Inspecting and maintaining equipment.
- Inspecting and maintaining snaplinks.
- Inspecting and maintaining rappelling gloves.
- Inspecting and maintaining rappel ropes.
- Identifying the rappel capabilities of aircraft used.
- Controlling rappels from UH-1H or UH-60 aircraft.
- Tying knots (square, bowline, half-hitch, Prusik), safety lines, and rappel seats (Swiss seat, Australian seat).
- Inspecting a rappel seat.
- Aircraft rigging for rappelling operations.
- Aircraft command and control.

PROFICIENCY MAINTENANCE

1-5. To remain current, rappel masters must execute their duties in a tactical or training exercise once every six months. If rappel masters do not execute their duties once every six months, they must take a refresher class taught by a current rappel master. The refresher class includes subjects listed in the rappel master qualifications listed above.

RAPPEL MASTER ON-SITE TRAINING REQUIREMENTS

1-6. Units may conduct ground training and wall-side tower rappelling without a school-trained rappel master as long the following requirement is met:
- A fully qualified rappel safety officer (RSO) is on site to assume the duties and responsibilities of the rappel master. The RSO must be certified and appointed by the commander.

RAPPEL SAFETY OFFICER

1-7. The RSO serves as the OIC during all rappel operations. Holding the rank of SFC or above, he is trained on applicable rappel master tasks and is certified by his commander to serve in the position. Extensive training in rappel operations and risk management, or graduation from one of the following courses are RSO requirements: Rappel Master Course; Air-assault Course, Ranger Course, Basic Military Mountaineering Course (summer or winter).

SAFETY

1-8. The RSO is responsible for the overall safety of all rappellers and ensures that all safety precautions are followed.

BRIEFINGS

1-9. The RSO briefs VIPs, visitors, and inspecting authorities on training, safety requirements, and layout of training areas.

RAPPEL LANE NCO

DUTIES AND RESPONSIBILITIES

1-10. Safety is the rappel lane NCO's number one priority. The rappel lane NCO—
- Ensures proper safety procedures are followed.
- Ensures proper hookup once directed to a rope station.
- Issues commands and maintains eye contact with the rappeller at all times.

QUALIFICATIONS

1-11. The rappel lane NCO is a commander-appointed corporal or above who is trained in the safe and proper execution of rappelling operations. Each tower rappel lane must have a qualified rappel lane NCO to supervise lane operations.

TRAINING

1-12. The rappel lane NCO must also be trained on the following subjects:
- Responsibilities and safety requirements.
- Inspection and maintenance of equipment.
- Identification of satisfactory anchor points.
- Identification of safe and unsafe hookups.
- Establishment of a rappel point.
- Inspection of a rappel seat.
- Coaching techniques.
- Rappelling procedures.
- Emergency procedures.
- Belay control procedures.

PROFICIENCY MAINTENANCE

1-13. If a rappel lane NCO has not conducted his duties within the last six months, he must complete the training listed in paragraph 1-12 under the supervision of a current rappel master.

RAPPELLER

1-14. Participants in tower rappel training must complete the following requirements under the supervision of a rappel master. The unit commander ensures that personnel successfully complete these requirements before beginning aircraft rappel training. Individual rappellers must—
- Identify all rappelling equipment.
- Demonstrate construction of rappel seat; donning of rappel harness; proper use and hook-up of rappel device and rappel rope.
- Identify unsafe attachments, equipment, rope connections, and seat construction.

Chapter 1

- Define terms used in rappelling operations.
- Identify knots used in rappel operations.
- Understand and demonstrate rappel commands.
- Demonstrate rappelling positions.
- Demonstrate belaying procedures.
- Exhibit satisfactory performance from a rappel tower of at least 34 feet in height (two rappels with equipment and weapon, two without equipment and weapon). Two rappels are conducted from the free side of the tower (no wall).
- Demonstrate the ability to lock-in.

BELAYER

1-15. Belay requirements are a subtask of basic rappel requirements. Soldiers must be trained to belay before conducting rappelling training. The belayer—

- Assumes a position at the base of the lane about one pace away from the tower area.
- Ensures that the rappel ropes are even with the ground during tower rappels.
- Loosely holds the rappel rope with both hands to avoid interference with the rappeller while remaining able to stop the rappeller should he fall.
- Immediately stops the rappeller by pulling downward on the rappel ropes if the rappeller shouts, FALLING! or loses control of his brake hand during descent.
- Watches the rappeller at all times, and maintains constant voice or visual contact.
- Wears a helmet to prevent injuries from falling debris.

BELAY SAFETY

1-16. The belay safety must be ranger or air assault qualified. He ensures belay personnel are performing their duties properly. Rappel training requires one belay safety for each two rappel stations. The belay safety must possess the same qualifications as a rappel lane NCO. He ensures belay personnel are performing their duties properly. Rappel training requires one belay safety for each two rappel stations.

SECTION II — PREOPERATIONS BRIEFINGS AND SAFETY PROCEDURES

1-17. The rappel master ensures participants have a basic understanding of requirements and safety procedures before conducting training.

SAFETY

1-18. The following personnel and equipment must be present during static tower training:

- Two military rappel ropes for each rappel station.
- One safety officer.
- One rappel master for each rappel site.
- One rappel lane NCO per rappel station.
- One medic with medical kit and backboard.
- One safety or medical evacuation vehicle with driver.
- One belayer for each rope station. Rappellers alternate stations.
- One belay safety for each two rappel stations (four ropes).

SAFETY BRIEFING

1-19. As in all training, a safety briefing precedes rappel operations. The rappel master briefs all personnel on safety to include the following instructions:

- Each rappeller ensures loose clothing and equipment are secured.

- Rappel seats are tied (or harnesses donned) by the Soldier and inspected by the rappel master before climbing the tower. Rappel seats are removed upon completion of every rappel. They are then retied and reinspected by a qualified rappel master or rappel lane NCO before subsequent rappels.
- Rappellers climb the tower only when directed by the rappel master or rappel lane NCO.
- Rappellers stay in the center of the tower until instructed to move to a rappel point.
- If using a troop ladder, only three Soldiers are on the ladder at one time. Soldiers do not climb the ladder until directed to do so by a rappel master.
- All personnel working within 3 feet of the edge of the top of the tower must wear a restraining strap, safety rope attached to the anchor, or safety rope attached to the rappel rope with break applied. No one is allowed within 3 feet of the tower's top edge without being secured.
- No one should lean or sit on the railing or banisters of the tower.
- When attaching the rappel rope to the snaplink, rappellers pull the slack toward the anchor point. The rappel master or rappel lane NCO physically check each hookup.
- All personnel weighing more than 200 pounds will conduct a standard hookup rappel to determine if they require a friction hookup. A friction hookup is created by placing an additional two ropes in the gate of the snaplink (for a total of six ropes in the snaplink).
- Combat equipment is positioned on the rappeller so it does not interfere with the brake hand. The weapon must be slung diagonally across the back with the muzzle pointing down, and on the opposite side of the brake hand.
- Heavy duty gloves are required for all rappel training.
- Ballistic or safety helmets with chin straps fastened are worn during tower rappel training.
- While on the tower, the rappeller maintains eye contact with the rappel master or rappel lane NCO and receives all commands from them.
- The rappeller ensures that he has a belayer on his rope.
- The belayer keeps both hands on the rope at all times. He also faces the rappeller at all times.
- All tower rappelling is performed with a double strand of rope.
- No running is allowed on the tower.
- No smoking or eating is allowed near the tower.
- All participants who are unable to rappel, lack confidence, or refuse to rappel are reported to the rappel master or OIC. These participants are immediately removed from the training area.
- The RSO and rappel master must be aware of the overconfidence and carelessness of some rappellers. The rappel master ensures all personnel are tower qualified before beginning aircraft rappel training.

TOWER SAFETY AND PREPARATION

1-20. The rappel master is in charge of the tower. He conducts a visual and physical inspection of every item of equipment including the structural lumber and timber, the ladder, the platform floor, and all anchor points.

- The static tower will not be used during thunderstorms or excessively high winds. If ice is present, or if the platform is slick from rain, rappelling will be delayed until conditions are safe.
- All rope stations are rigged with two anchor points (Figure 1-2 A, B, C). The first anchor point is a middle-of-the-rope knot; the second is an end-of-the-rope anchor knot. The rappel master removes all slack between the knots to create equal tension on the anchor points. He also ensures rappel ropes reach all the way to the ground.

Chapter 1

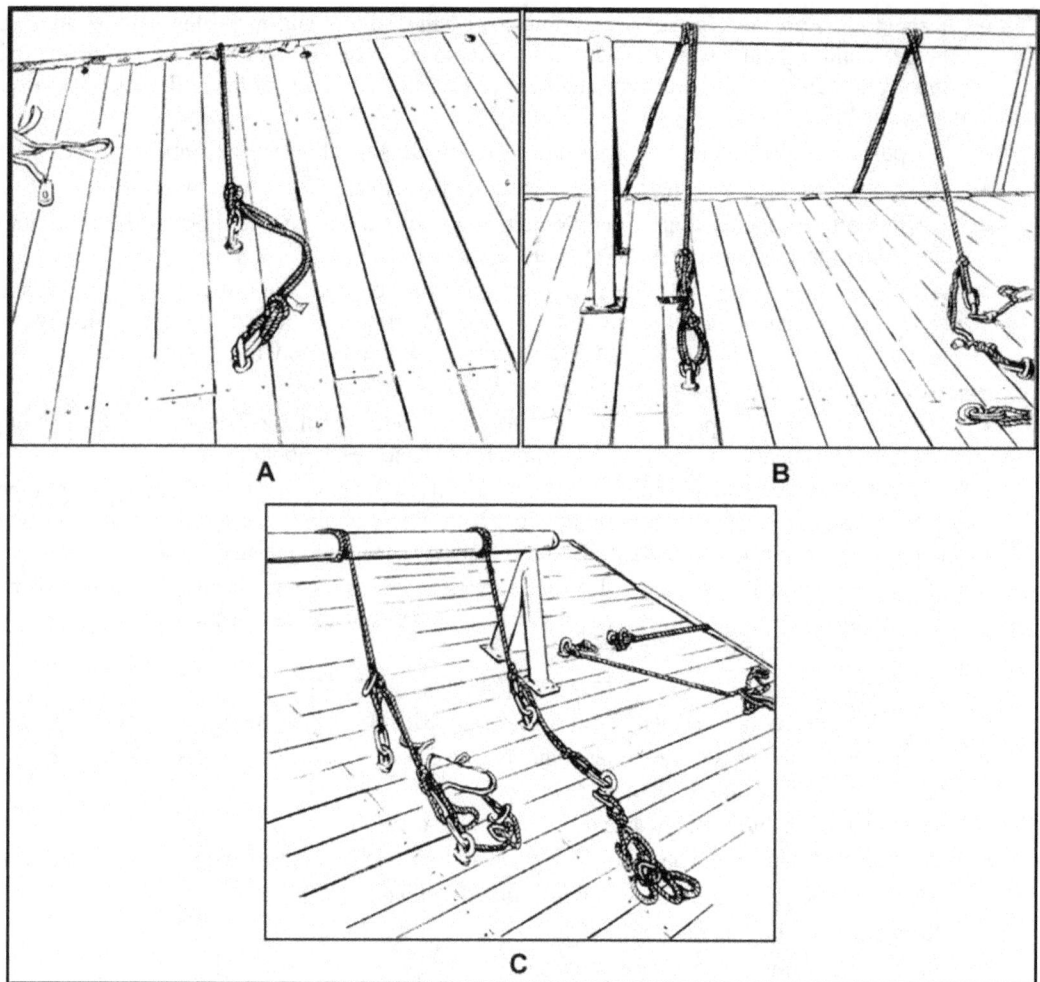

Figure 1-2. Example of rappel tower anchor points.

RAPPELLER PREPARATION

1-21. Before conducting a rappel each rappeller must prepare his individual clothing and equipment. Strict attention must be paid to the following:

> **WARNING**
>
> **Failure to properly prepare rappellers could result in bodily injury or damage to equipment.**

- Secure shirt tails, loose clothing, equipment, straps, and long hair.
- Wear a helmet during rappelling. Properly fasten all straps and ensure the helmet is in serviceable condition.
- Wear heavy leather workman's gloves.
- Wear identification tags.

Tower Rappelling

- When rappelling with equipment, load-bearing equipment (LBE) or load-bearing vests (LBV) should be unfastened in the front or fastened loosely behind the back of the rappeller. The rucksack should be worn high and tight on the back of the rappeller to allow the brake hand to reach the small of the back. Rucksack adjustment straps will be tied across the chest or tucked away.
- Sling the weapon diagonally across the back with the muzzle down. Ensure the muzzle is on the guide-hand side and the stock is toward the brake hand.

NOTE: Soldiers rappelling with equipment in excess of 50 pounds may want to consider using a friction hookup.

SECTION III — RAPPELLING PROCEDURES

1-22. This section discusses procedures used in tower rappelling.

SEAT-HIP RAPPEL

1-23. When using the seat-hip rappel, friction is created by a snaplink that is inserted in a sling rope seat and fastened to the rappeller. This method provides a faster and more controlled descent than other methods. Wear gloves to prevent rope burns. An alternate technique is to insert a second snaplink into the first snaplink (attached to rappel seat) and run the rope through the second snaplink. This allows easier disengagement from the rappel rope without running the entire rope through the first snaplink. To disengage from the rappel rope using the alternate technique, release the tension from the rope by opening the gate of the first snaplink and removing the second snaplink (with the rope attached).

THE RAPPEL SEAT

1-24. The rappel seat is constructed as follows (Figure 1-3 A through 1-3 T):

(1) Place the midpoint (center) of the length of the sling rope on the hip opposite the brake hand (the brake hand is the strong hand) (Figure 1-3 A, B, C).
(2) Bring the sling rope around the waist above the hip bone. Tie a double overhand knot over the navel (Figure 1-3 D, E, F, G, H).
(3) Let the two free ends of the sling rope fall to the ground in front (Figure 1-3 I).
(4) Bring the two free ends of the sling rope down between the legs and up over the buttocks. Ensure that the two free ends do not cross (Figure 1-3 J).
(5) Pass the ends of the ropes over the rope that is tied around the waist at the two points above the center of the two rear seat pockets (Figure 1-3 K).
(6) Grab the free end of the rope that is on the left side of the body with the left hand, and the free end of the rope that is on the right side of the body with the right hand.
(7) Squat down and simultaneously pull on both running ends of the ropes and stand up. This will tighten the seat.
(8) Take the two running ends of the rope down and back over the waist rope from the inside. Bring the running ends back under the ropes that are going across the buttocks (Figure 1-3 L).
(9) Tie the two running ends with a square knot and two overhand knots on the hip opposite the brake hand (Figure 1-3 M, N).
(10) Place any excess rope in the trouser pocket near the square knot (Figure 1-3 O, P).
(11) With the gate down and the hooked end of the snaplink against the navel, place the end of the snaplink through the single rope that is around the waist and the two ropes forming the double-hand knot (Figure 1-3 Q).
(12) Rotate the snaplink a half turn so the gate is facing up and will open away from the body (Figure 1-3 R, S, T).

Chapter 1

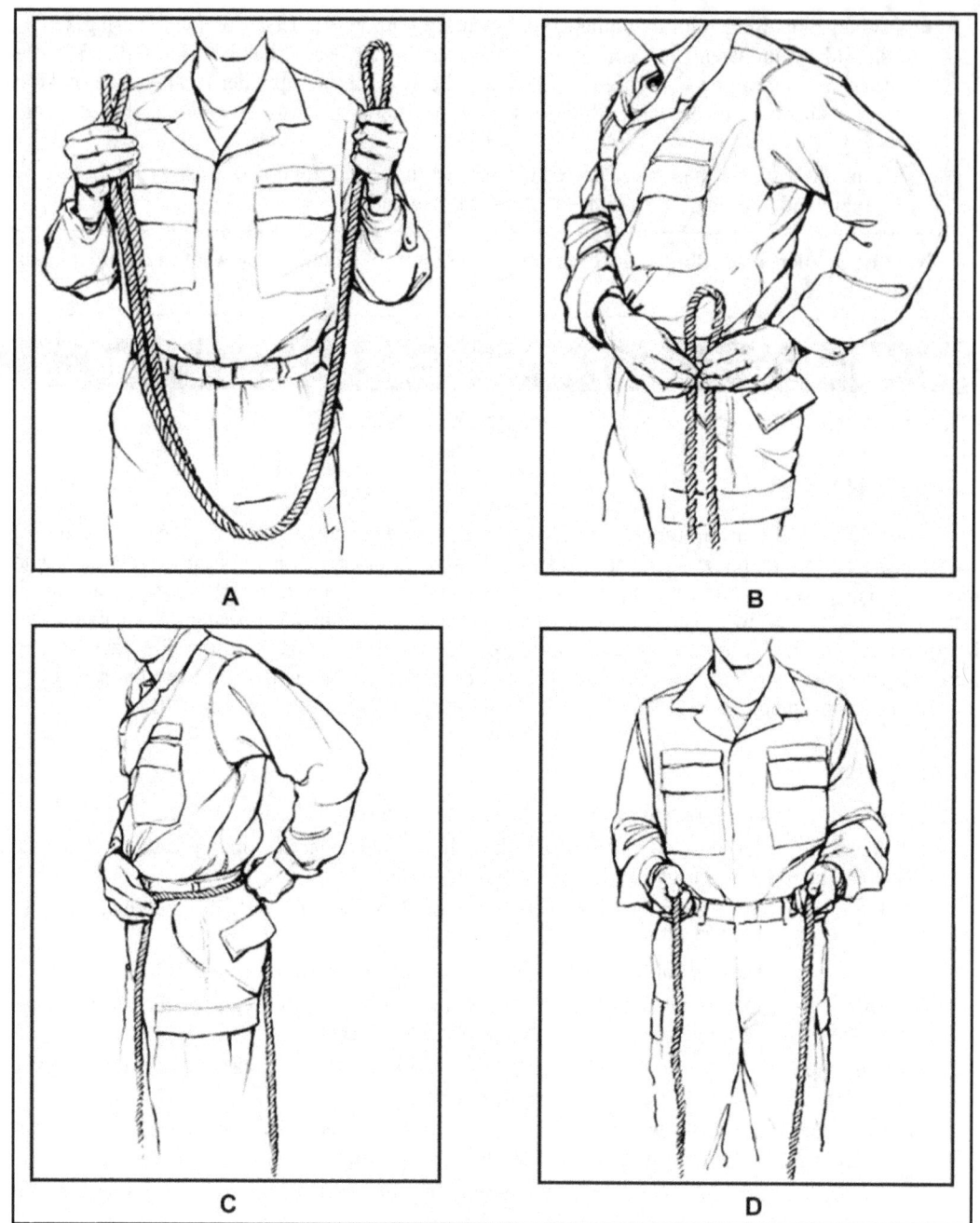

Figure 1-3. Construction of rappel seat.

Tower Rappelling

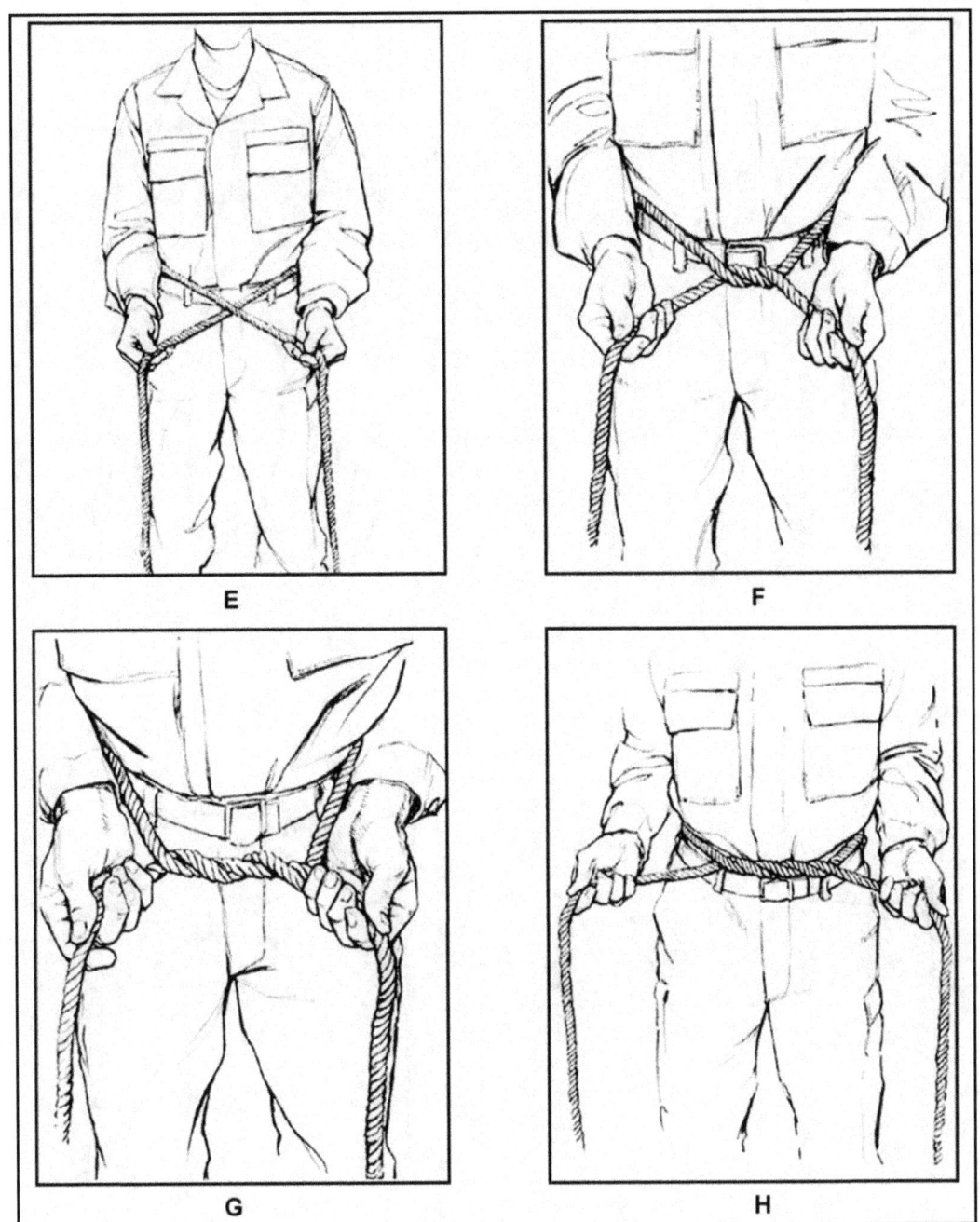

Figure 1-3. Construction of rappel seat (continued).

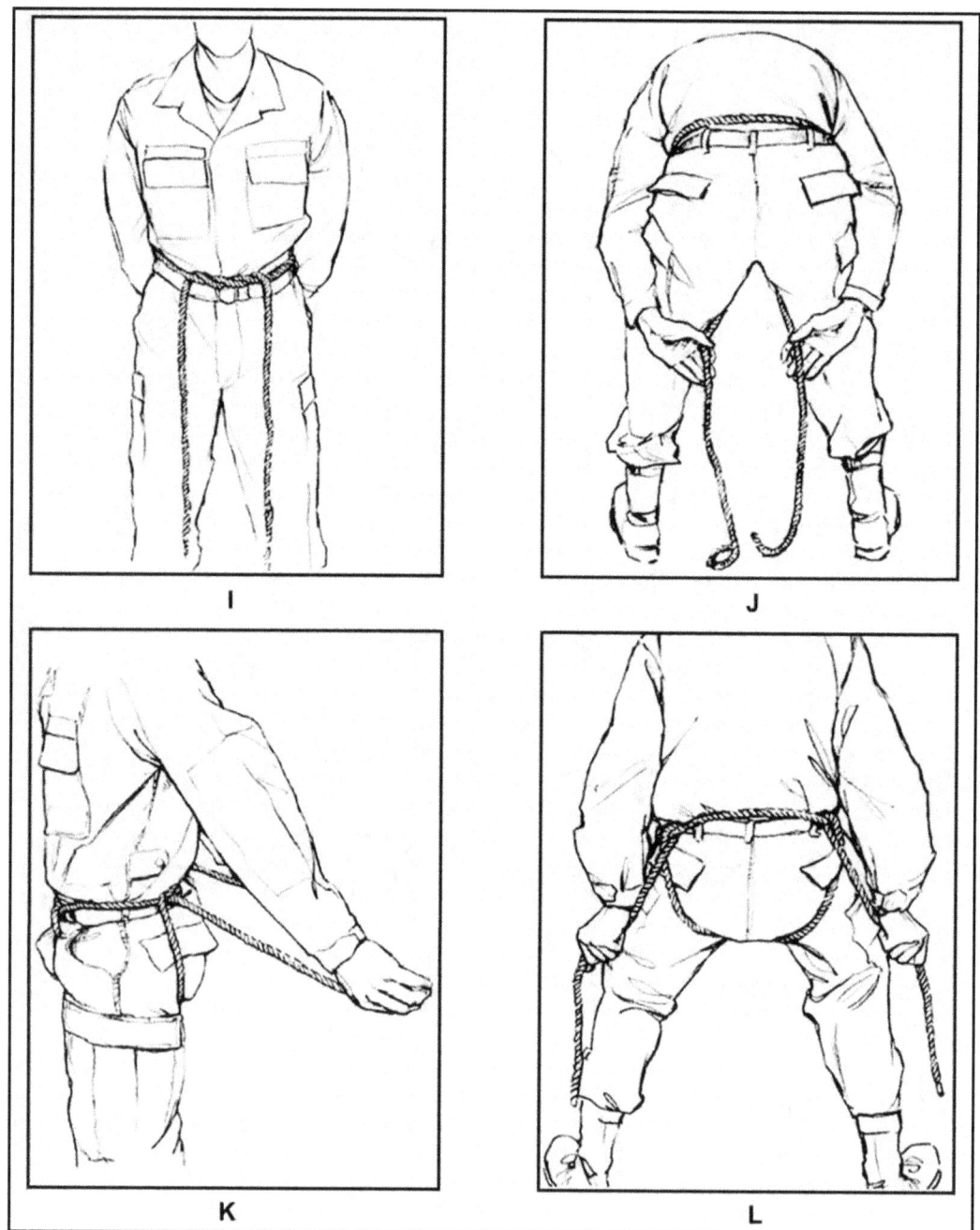

Figure 1-3. Construction of rappel seat (continued).

Tower Rappelling

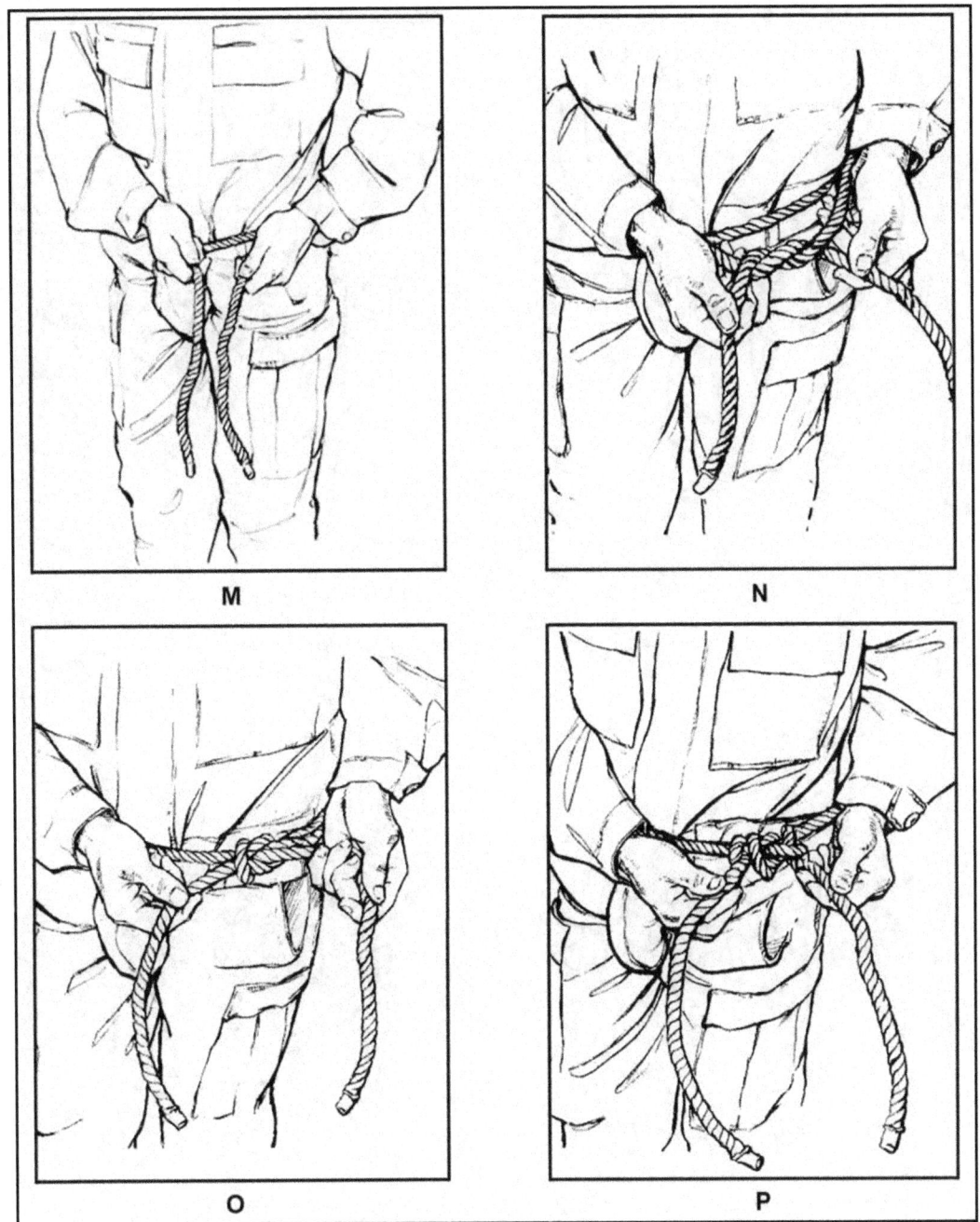

Figure 1-3. Construction of rappel seat (continued).

Chapter 1

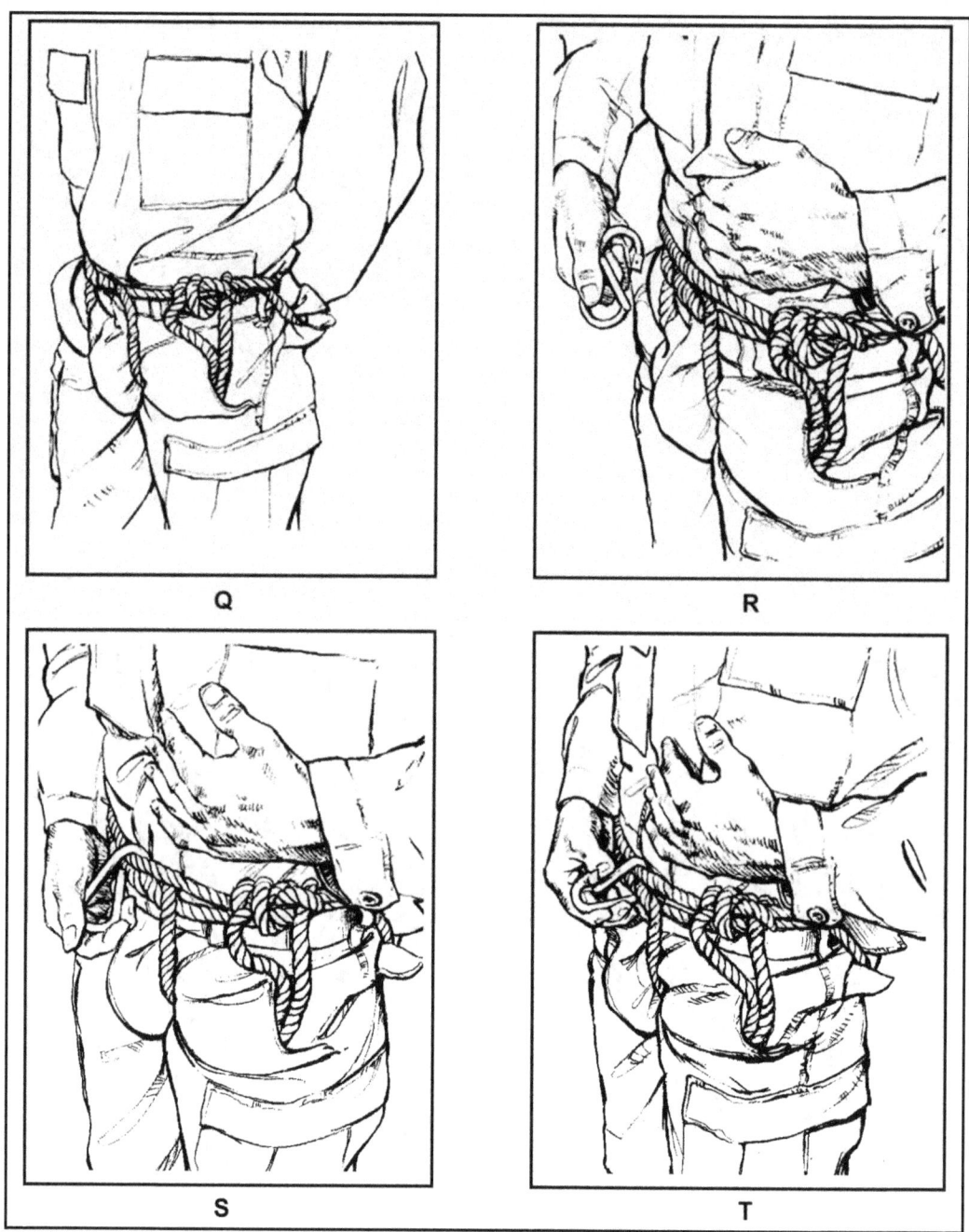

Figure 1-3. Construction of rappel seat (continued).

HOOK UP

1-25. To hook up using the seat-hip method, perform the following:
- Place the square knot with two overhand knots toward the anchor point for all seat-hip rappels.
- Grasp the two ropes with both hands and drop them through the gate of the snaplink. (At this point, two ropes should be running through the snaplink.)
- Using the hand closest to the anchor point, pull the slack toward the anchor point. Rotate the slack under and then over the top of the snaplink.
- Drop the two ropes a second time through the gate of the snaplink. (At this point, four ropes should be running through the snaplink.)

- Place the guide hand on the rope between the anchor point and the snaplink (palm facing up).
- Place the brake hand around the running end of the rope (palm facing down). Place the brake hand with the rope in the small of the back.

AUSTRALIAN RAPPEL

1-26. To hook up for the Australian rappel (Figure 1-4), perform the following:

(1) Hook up to the Australian seat.
- Grasp the 9-foot sling rope at the midpoint (center) of its length, and double the rope.
- Place the doubled sling rope around the back and waist. Ensure that the rope is above the hipbone, but below the ribs.
- Tie a square knot with two overhand knots over the navel.
- Place any excess rope in the trouser pocket nearest the excess.

(2) When the Australian seat is donned, face away from the anchor point and to the side of the rappel rope. (Stand to the same side of the rope as the brake hand. Determine left and right of the rope while facing the anchor point.) Place a snaplink onto the seat with the gate facing up, hinge closest to the body. Place it on the hip corresponding to the brake hand. The rappel master grasps the rappel rope and lays the rope into the snaplink. He then places one hand between the snaplink and the anchor point and draws slack toward the anchor point. He rotates the slack down, under, and over the rope and into the snaplink. The rappel master then slides the snaplink directly to the rappeller's back.

(3) Serve the running end of the rappel rope with the brake hand and prepare to rappel. During descent, brake by drawing the rappel ropes diagonally across the chest with the ropes running from near the waist to the pocket of the opposite shoulder.

Figure 1-4. Australian rappel.

CLIMBING PROCEDURES

1-27. Before climbing the ladder, the rappel master, safety OIC, or rappel lane NCO checks each rappeller's equipment.
- The rappeller kicks the sand off his boots before climbing.
- The rappeller grasps the outside of the ladder while climbing, not the rungs (when possible). If stairs are built for the tower, the rappeller grasps the railings as appropriate.

Chapter 1

- Just before climbing up the ladder, the rappeller sounds off, (NAME) CLIMBING, and then begins climbing up the ladder. Once at the top and clear of the ladder, the rappeller sounds off, (NAME) CLEAR.
- Once off the ladder, the rappeller waits until the rappel master or lane NCO directs him to proceed to a rope station. At this time, the next rappeller in line may start to climb the ladder.

TOWER PROCEDURES

1-28. After the rappellers climb the tower, the following procedures are adhered to:
- Once directed to a rope station, the rappel master or lane NCO ensures proper hookup for rappelling.
- At this time, the rappeller sounds off with ON RAPPEL and the belayer sounds off with ON BELAY.
- While maintaining his brake, the rappeller (on command from the rappel master or lane NCO) steps over the safety rail and faces the anchor point.
- At this point, the rappel lane NCO sounds off with the following verbal commands and arm-and-hand signals.

TOWER PROCEDURES ARM AND HAND SIGNALS

(1) *Get Ready*—Rappel master or lane NCO extends both arms to the front with fists clenched and thumbs pointing upward (Figure 1-5). This alerts the rappeller. Each rappeller looks over his brake hand shoulder to check for the belay man. The rappeller then looks at the rappel master. The rappel master or lane NCO makes his second check of the hookup, rappel seat, snaplink, and equipment.

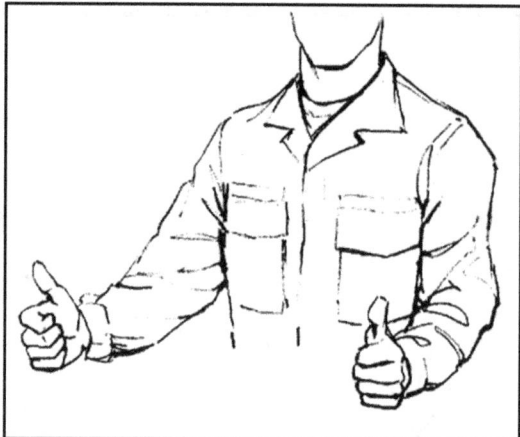

Figure 1-5. Example of arm-and-hand signal GET READY.

(2) *Position*—The lane NCO extends both arms to the front, elbows locked, forearms pointed downward, and fingers extended. He makes a circular motion with both forearms rotating in opposite directions (Figure 1-6). With the brake hand in the small of the back, the rappeller rotates 180 degrees out onto the wall or skid mock up and assumes an L-shaped position. The feet should be shoulder width apart, balls of feet on the wall or skid, knees locked, and body bent at the waist (Figure 1-7).

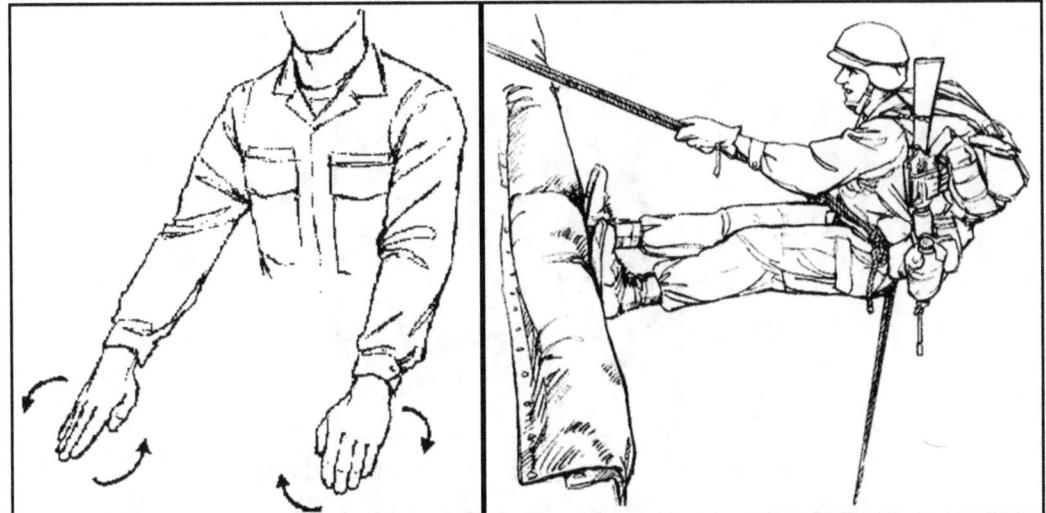

Figure 1-6. Example of arm-and-hand signal POSITION.

Figure 1-7. L-shape position.

    (3) *Go*—The lane NCO extends his right arm with the elbow locked, fingers extended, thumbs around the index fingers, and points directly at the rappeller (Figure 1-8). This initiates the rappel. The rappeller flexes his knees and jumps vigorously backward. At the same time, the rappeller throws his brake hand out at a 45-degree angle, letting the rope slide through both the brake hand and the guide hand. The rappeller looks over his brake hand shoulder at all times during descent.

Figure 1-8. Example of arm-and-hand signal GO.

- The rappeller descends in a smooth, controlled manner.
- The rappeller maintains eye contact with the ground at all times.
- The rappeller maintains a modified L-shape position during descent with the feet shoulder-width apart, knees flexed, and buttocks parallel to the ground (Figure 1-9).

Chapter 1

Figure 1-9. L-shape position while rappelling.

- When carrying equipment or additional weight, a modified L-shape is used with the legs slightly lower than the buttocks to compensate for the added weight.
- The rappeller's back is straight. He looks over the brake hand shoulder.
- The guide hand is extended on the rope with the elbow extended and locked.
- The rope slides freely through the guide hand, which is used to adjust equipment and to assist balance during descent.
- To brake, the rappeller places the brake hand (with rope in hand) in the small of the back and then grasps the rope firmly with the brake hand.

NOTE: Do not grip the rope firmly with the brake hand while the brake hand and brake arm are extended at the 45-degree angle. If this is done while rappelling, the brake hand and glove may become entangled in the snaplink causing injury to the hand and causing the rappeller to become hung up on the ropes.

- Releasing tension on the rope and moving the brake hand out to the rear at a 45-degree angle regulates the rate of descent.
- The rappeller never lets go of the rope with his brake hand until the rappel is completed.
- After the rope is cleared and the rappeller is off rappel, he acts as the belayer for the next rappeller.

RAPPEL TOWER TRAINING FOR THE UH-1H HELICOPTER

1-29. Training on the rappel tower for helicopter skid rappelling prepares Soldiers to rappel from a UH-1H helicopter (Figure 1-10).

1-30. The rappeller is hooked up while he sits on the platform just above the helicopter skid. On the rappel master's command, GET READY, the rappeller looks over the edge of the tower to ensure the running ends of the ropes are on the ground (Figure 1-10 A).

1-31. On the command, SIT IN THE DOOR, the rappeller rotates his feet and legs off the platform and places them on the skid (Figure 1-10 B).

1-32. On the command, POSITION, the rappeller turns around and assumes an L-shape position (Figure 1-10 C).

1-33. On the command, GO, the rappeller bounds away from the helicopter skid and rappels to the ground. The rappel master is responsible for the proper procedures and safety.

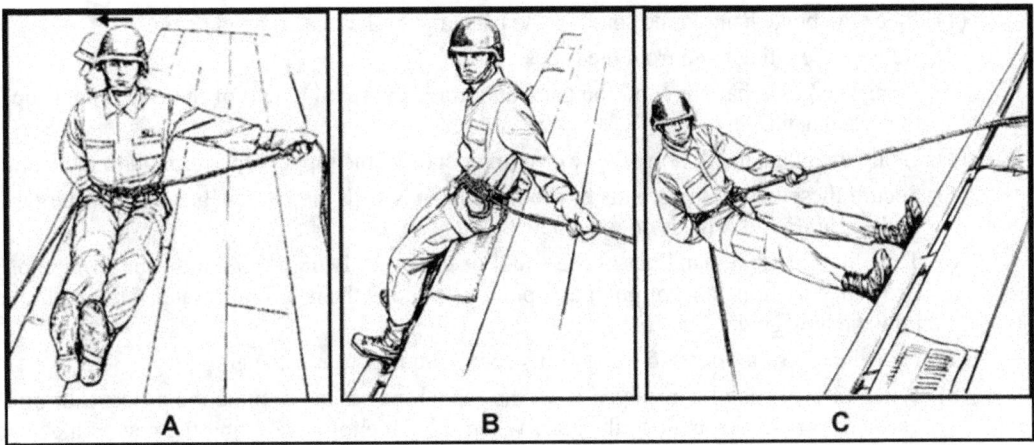

Figure 1-10. UH-1H helicopter skid rappel training.

RAPPEL TOWER TRAINING FOR THE UH-60 BLACKHAWK HELICOPTER

1-34. Rappel tower training for the UH-60 Blackhawk is similar to that for the UH-1H with the exception that the UH-60 has no skids on which to stand. Therefore, the edge of the rappel tower is used as a pivot point to assume the L-shape position. All commands are the same except for SIT IN THE DOOR, which does not apply to the UH-60. The stances for each command are also different, as shown in Figure 1-11 A, B.

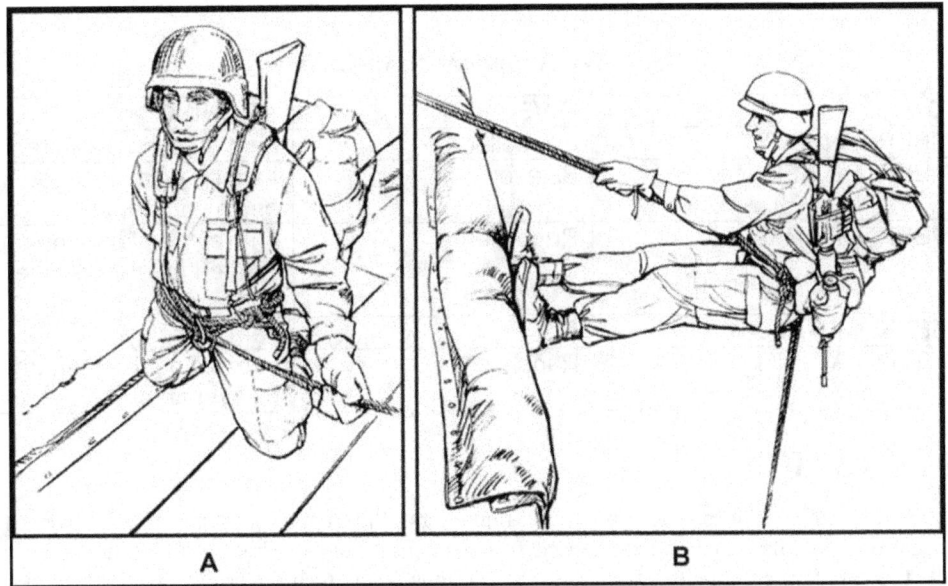

Figure 1-11. UH-60 helicopter rappel training.

EMERGENCY LOCK-IN PROCEDURES

1-35. Mastering the lock-in procedure during tower training is critical before advancing to helicopter rappelling. Using the lock-in procedure allows personnel to hold in position for an extended period of time.

1-36. If the helicopter gains altitude above the length of the rappel ropes, the rappeller immediately brakes, locks-in, and waits for the descent of the aircraft. Procedures for lock-in are as follows:

Chapter 1

(1) Place the brake hand in the small of the back and brake to a complete stop.

(2) Release the guide hand from the ropes.

(3) Bring the guide hand around the back and grasp the running end of the two rappel ropes behind the brake hand.

(4) Using the guide hand, bring the two running ends of the rappel ropes around to the front.

(5) Secure these two running ends of the rappel ropes with the two anchor ends of the rappel ropes in the guide hand. This is now the new brake hand.

(6) Take the old brake hand out of the small of the back. Bring it around to the front and grasp the two ropes from the anchor point at a point just above the new brake hand. The old brake hand is now the new guide hand.

(7) Face the rappel master and wait for his command to lower to the ground.

(8) When the command is received from the rappel master to continue the descent, bring the brake hand to a 45-degree angle to the rear. When it is time to brake, bring the new brake hand around to the front diagonally across the chest.

1-37. If an engine fails or an aircraft emergency occurs during rappelling, the rappellers on the ropes descend as rapidly as possible and move from beneath the aircraft to the sides. If possible, rappellers will maintain control of ropes.

COMMUNICATIONS

1-38. The rappeller at the top of a rappel point must be able to communicate with those at the bottom. Radios, hand signals, and rope signals are considered during a tactical rappel. For training situations, use the commands in Table 1-1.

Table 1-1. Rappeller commands.

COMMAND	GIVEN BY	MEANING
LANE NUMBER, ON RAPPEL	Rappeller	I am ready to begin rappelling.
LANE NUMBER, ON BELAY	Belayer	I am on belay and you may begin your rappel.
LANE NUMBER, OFF RAPPEL	Rappeller	I have completed the rappel, cleared the rappel lane, and am off the rope.
LANE NUMBER, OFF BELAY	Belayer	I am off belay.
LANE NUMBER, FALLING	Rappeller	I am falling. Be alert below—belay man brake.

DEMONSTRATION

1-39. After explaining the procedures to all rappellers, the rappel master should have an assistant demonstrate one complete cycle of rappelling from the static tower. This ensures that the rappellers can hear all the proper commands and see the actions and techniques used on the static tower.

Chapter 2
GROUND RAPPELLING

Ground rappelling is a technique that allows Soldiers to negotiate mountains and cliffs safely and rapidly. Before rappellers participate in mountain and cliff rappelling they should complete all requirements for tower training.

PERSONNEL

2-1. The personnel responsibilities for mountain and cliff rappelling are the same as for tower rappelling. As a minimum the following personnel are needed for mountain and cliff rappelling.

MOUNTAINEERING SAFETY OFFICER

2-2. The mountaineering safety officer (MSO) is a SFC or above appointed by the commander. He is ranger qualified; is a graduate of the Basic Military Mountaineering Course (Level I Mountaineer) and Assault Climber Course (Level II Mountaineer); or is extensively trained in ground rappelling. He has overall responsibility for the safety of all mountaineering participants and ensures that all safety precautions are followed.

RAPPEL POINT COMMANDER

2-3. The rappel point commander is a ranger qualified NCO. His qualifications may include graduation from the Basic Military Mountaineering (Level I Mountaineer) and Assault Climber Courses (Level II Mountaineer). The rappel point commander has overall responsibility for establishing and running the ground rappel points. He ensures that the rope anchors are sound and the knots are tied properly. He also clears loose rock and debris from the loading platform, and ensures that the rappel point is run safely.

RAPPEL LANE NCO

2-4. The rappel lane NCO is a qualified officer or NCO in charge of rappel lane on a wall or ground rappel.

SUSTAINMENT TRAINING

2-5. Before conducting ground rappel training, the unit or element conducts sustainment training. Training should include the following:
- Review the construction of a rappel seat, seats to be used, and hook-up procedures.
- Conduct a minimum of one rappel on the 34-foot tower wall (20-foot tower is acceptable) under the same conditions as ground rappelling. If conducting ground rappelling with combat equipment, it is recommended that Soldiers conduct two tower rappels; one with equipment, one without equipment.
- Demonstrate the ability to lock-in during one of the rappels from the free side of the tower.

SELECTION OF A RAPPEL POINT

2-6. The selection of the rappel point depends on factors such as mission, cover, route, anchor points, and edge composition (loose or jagged rocks). The anchor point should be above the rappeller's departure point. Anchors must be solid (natural anchors are preferred). The rappeller should be sure that the rope reaches the bottom or a place from which he can further rappel or climb. Also, the rappel point should be carefully tested and inspected to ensure the rope will run freely, and that the area is clear of obstacles that could be dislodged. Suitable loading and off-loading platforms should be available.

ESTABLISHMENT OF A RAPPEL ANCHOR POINT

2-7. Proper selection and placement of anchors is a critical skill that requires a great deal of practice. Failure of any system will probably occur at the anchor point. If the anchor is not strong enough to support the intended load, it will fail. Failure is usually the result of poor terrain features selected for the anchor point, the improper placement of anchor-rigging equipment, or an improper amount of anchor-rigging equipment. When selecting or constructing anchors, always make sure the anchor is "bombproof". A bombproof anchor is stronger than any possible load that could be placed on it. An anchor that has more strength than the rappel rope is considered bombproof.

NATURAL ANCHORS

2-8. Natural anchors should be considered for use first. They are usually strong and often simple to construct with minimal use of equipment. Trees, boulders, and other terrain irregularities are already in place and simply require a method for attaching the rope. However, natural anchors should be carefully studied and evaluated for stability and strength before use. Sometimes the rappelling rope is tied directly to the anchor, but under most circumstances a sling is attached to the anchor before a rappel rope is attached to the sling with a carabineer(s).

TYING THE RAPPEL ROPE

2-9. When tying the rappel rope around an anchor, the knot should be placed the same distance away from the anchor as the diameter of the anchor (Figure 2-1). The knot should not be placed up against the anchor because this can stress and distort the knot under tension.

Figure 2-1. Rope tied to anchor with anchor knot.

Ground Rappelling

ARTIFICIAL ANCHORS

2-10. Artificial anchors are used when natural anchors are unavailable. The art of choosing and placing good anchors requires extensive training and experience. Only Level II mountaineers are authorized to establish artificial anchors. Artificial anchors are available in many different types. The type used depends on the terrain, equipment, and load to be placed on it.

EQUALIZED ANCHORS

2-11. Equalized anchors are made up of more than one anchor point joined together so the intended load is shared equally. This not only provides greater anchor strength, but adds redundancy or backup because of the multiple points.

Self-equalizing Anchor

2-12. A self-equalizing anchor will maintain an equal load on each individual point as the direction of pull changes (Figure 2-2). This is sometimes used in rappelling when the route must change left or right in the middle of the rappel. A self-equalizing anchor should only be used when necessary, because if any one of the individual points fail, the anchor will extend and shock-load the remaining points. It may even cause complete anchor failure.

Figure 2-2. Self-equalizing anchors.

Pre-equalized Anchor

2-13. A pre-equalized anchor distributes the load equally to each individual point (Figure 2-3). It is aimed in the direction of the load. A pre-equalized anchor prevents extension and shock-loading of the anchor if

Chapter 2

an individual point fails. An anchor is pre-equalized by tying an overhand or figure-eight knot in the webbing or sling.

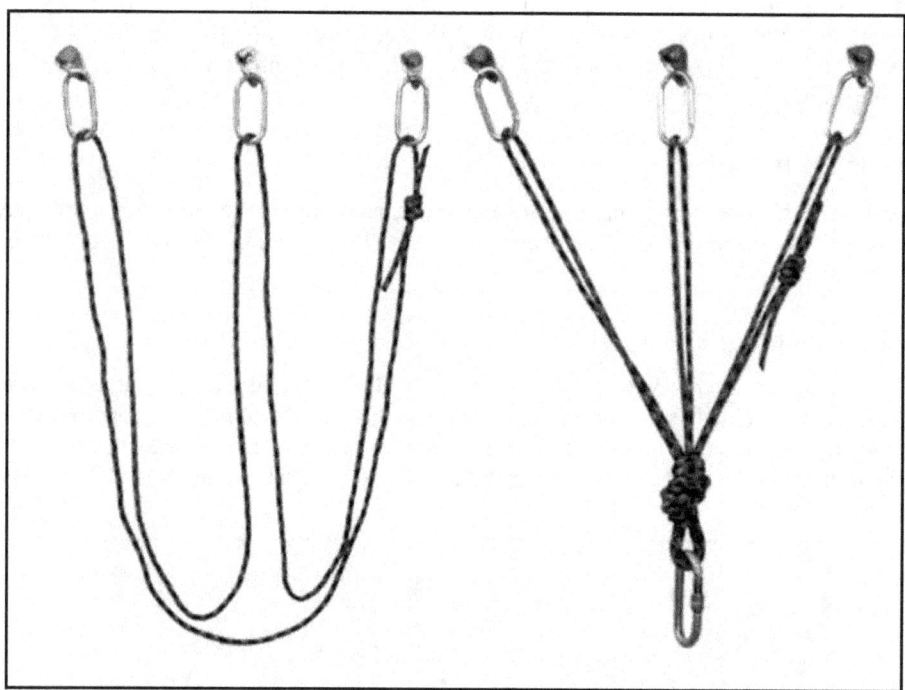

Figure 2-3. Pre-equalized anchor.

NOTE: When using webbing or slings, the angles of the webbing or slings directly affect the load placed on an anchor. An angle greater than 90-degrees can result in anchor failure (Figure 2-4).

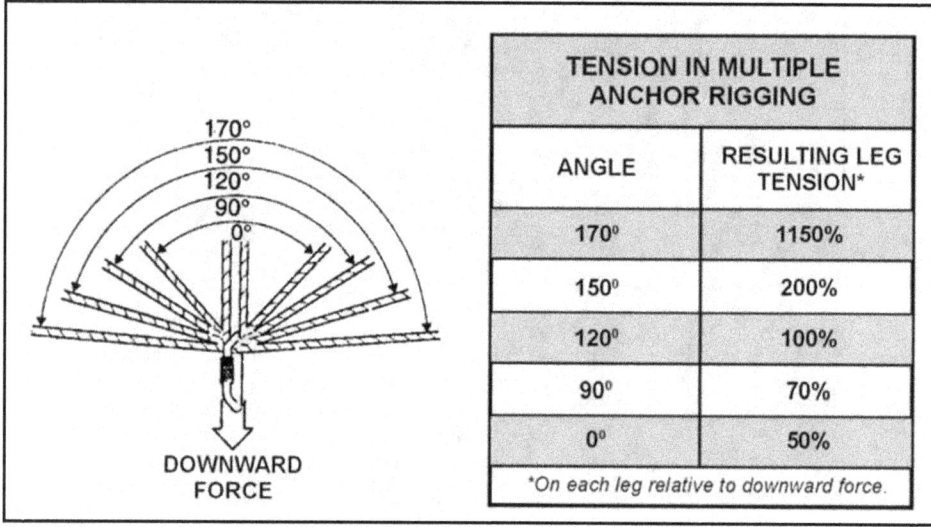

Figure 2-4. Effects of angles on an anchor.

ESTABLISHING THE RAPPEL LANE

2-14. Once the anchor has been selected and established, the rappel rope is attached to the anchor and the lane is established. If a rappel lane is less than half the rope length, the climber may apply one of the

following techniques:
- Double the rope and tie a three-loop bowline around the primary anchor to include the primary anchor inside two loops and enough rope in the third loop to run to the secondary anchor (another three-loop bowline secured with an overhand knot).
- Bowline secure with an overhand knot (or any appropriate anchor knot).
- Double the rope and establish a self-equalizing anchor system with a three-loop bowline or any other appropriate anchor knot

2-15. If a rappel lane is greater than half the rope length, the climber may apply one of the following techniques:
- Use two ropes. With both ropes, tie a round turn anchor bowline around a primary anchor point. Take the remaining rope (the tail from the primary anchor bowline) and tie another round turn anchor bowline to a secondary anchor point. The secondary anchor point should be in a direct line behind the primary anchor point. The anchor can be either natural or artificial.
- Use two ropes. Establish a multi-point anchor system using a bowline on a bight or any other appropriate anchor knot.

2-16. Situations may arise where, due to the length of the rappel, the rappel rope cannot be tied to the anchor. (If the rope is used to tie the knots, it will be too short to accomplish the rappel). The following techniques can be used:
- When using a natural anchor, tie a sling rope, piece of webbing, or another rope around the anchor using proper techniques for slinging natural anchors. The rappel rope will have a fixed loop tied in one end, which is attached to the anchor created.
- When using an artificial anchor, tie off a sling rope, piece of webbing, runner, or another rope to form a loop. Use this loop to create an equalizing or pre-equalized anchor, to which the rappel rope will be attached.

OPERATION OF THE RAPPEL POINT

2-17. Due to the inherent dangers of rappelling, special care must be taken to ensure a safe and successful descent.

COMMUNICATION

2-18. Climbers at the top of a rappel point must be able to communicate with those at the bottom. Radios, hand signals, and rope signals are all considered during a tactical rappel. For training situations use the commands shown in Table 2-1.

Table 2-1. Rappel commands.

COMMAND	GIVEN BY	MEANING
LANE NUMBER ___, ON RAPPEL	Rappeller	I am ready to begin rappelling.
LANE NUMBER ___, ON BELAY	Belayer	I am on belay and you may begin your rappel.
LANE NUMBER ___, OFF RAPPEL	Rappeller	I have completed the rappel, cleared the rappel lane, and am off the rope.
LANE NUMBER ___, OFF BELAY	Belayer	I am off belay.

Chapter 2

NOTES:

1. In a training environment, the lane number must be understood.

2. In a tactical situation, a series of tugs on the rope may be substituted for the oral commands to maintain noise discipline. The number of tugs used to indicate each command is IAW unit SOP.

DUTIES AND RESPONSIBILITIES

2-19. Duties of the rappel point commander follow:
- Ensures that the anchors are sound and the knots are properly tied.
- Ensures that loose rock and debris are cleared from the loading platform.
- Allows only one man on the loading platform at a time and ensures that the rappel point is run orderly.
- Ensures that each man is properly prepared for the particular rappel: gloves on, sleeves down, helmet with chin strap fastened, gear prepared properly, and rappel seat and knots correct (if required). Also ensures the rappeller is hooked up to the rope correctly and is aware of the proper braking position.
- Ensures that the proper signals or commands are used.
- Dispatches each man down the rope.
- Is the last man down the rope.

2-20. Duties of the first rappeller down follow:
- Selects a smooth route for the rope that is clear of sharp rocks.
- Conducts a self-belay.
- Clears the route placing loose rocks the rope may dislodge far enough back on ledges to be out of the way.
- Ensures the rope reaches the bottom or is at a place from which additional rappels can be made.
- Ensures that the rope will run freely around the rappel point when pulled from below.
- Clears the rappel lane by straightening all twists and tangles from the ropes.
- Belays subsequent rappellers down the rope or monitors subsequent belayers.
- Takes charge of personnel as they arrive at the bottom (off-loading platform).

NOTE: A rappeller is always belayed from the bottom, except for the first man down. The first man belays himself down the rope using a self-belay attached to his rappel seat, which is hooked to the rappel rope with a friction knot. As the first man rappels down the rope, he "walks" the friction knot down with him.

- Each rappeller down clears the ropes and shouts, OFF RAPPEL! (if the tactical situation permits). After the rope is cleared and the rappeller is off rappel, he acts as the belayer for next rappeller.
- Soldiers wear gloves for all types of rappels to protect their hands from rope burns.
- Rappellers descend in a smooth, controlled manner.

2-21. The body forms an L-shape with the feet shoulder-width apart, legs straight, and buttocks parallel to the ground. When carrying equipment or additional weight, a modified L-shape is used with the legs slightly lower than the buttocks to compensate for the additional weight. The rappeller's back is straight. He looks over the brake shoulder. The guide hand is extended on the rope with the elbow extended and locked. The rope slides freely through the guide hand. The guide hand is used to adjust equipment and assist balance during descent. The rappeller grasps the rope firmly with the brake hand and places it in the brake position. Releasing tension on the rope and moving the brake hand regulates the rate of descent. The rappeller never lets go of the ropes with his brake hand until the rappel is complete.

Ground Rappelling

TYING OFF DURING THE RAPPEL

2-22. It may be necessary to stop during descent. This can be accomplished by passing the rope around the body and placing three or more wraps around the guide-hand-side leg, or by tying off using the appropriate knot for the rappel device.

RECOVERY OF THE RAPPEL POINT

2-23. After assigned personnel have descended, only two personnel will remain at the top of the rappel point. They will be responsible for establishing a retrievable rappel.

ESTABLISHING THE RETRIEVABLE RAPPEL

2-24. To set up a retrievable rappel point, a climber must apply one of the following methods:

(1) Double the rope when the rappel is less than half the total length of the rope. Place the rope, with the bight formed by the midpoint, around the primary anchor. Join the tails of the rappel rope and throw the rope over the cliff. Tie a clove hitch around a carabiner, just below the anchor point, with the locking bar outside the carabiner away from the gate opening end and facing uphill. Snap the opposite standing portion into the carabiner. When the rappeller reaches the bottom, he pulls on that portion of the rope to which the carabiner is secured to allow the rope to slide around the anchor point.

(2) When the length of the rappel is greater than half the length of the rope used, join two ropes around the anchor point with an appropriate joining knot (except the square knot). Adjust the joining knot so it is away from the anchor. Tie a clove hitch around a carabiner just below the anchor point with the locking bar outside the carabiner away from the gate opening end and facing uphill. Snap the opposite standing portion into the carabiner. Upon completion of the rappel, pull the rope to which the carabiner is secured and allow the rope to slide around the anchor point.

NOTES:

1. When setting up a retrievable rappel, use only a primary point. Care should be taken when selecting the point.

2. Ensure the Soldiers have a safety line when approaching the rappel point, with only the rappeller going near the edge.

RETRIEVING THE RAPPEL ROPE

2-25. The next to last rappeller will descend the lane, removing any twists, and routes the rope for easiest retrieval. Once he reaches the end of the rappel, he tests the rope for retrieval. If the rappel is retrievable, the last man will rappel down. Once he is off rappel, he pulls the lane down.

TYPES OF RAPPELS

2-26. Many types of rappels may be used during military mountaineering operations. The following paragraphs describe some these rappels.

HASTY RAPPEL

2-27. The hasty rappel (Figure 2-5) is used only on moderate pitches. Its main advantage is it is easier and faster than other methods. Gloves are worn to prevent rope burns.

(1) Facing slightly sideways to the anchor, the rappeller places the ropes horizontally across his back. The hand nearest to the anchor is his guide hand; the other is his brake hand.

(2) To stop, the rappeller brings his brake hand across in front of his body locking the rope. At the same time, he turns to face up toward the anchor point.

Chapter 2

Figure 2-5. Hasty rappel.

BODY RAPPEL

2-28. During a body rappel (Figure 2-6), the rappeller faces the anchor point and straddles the rope. He then pulls the rope from behind, runs it around either hip, diagonally across the chest, and back over the opposite shoulder. From there, the rope runs to the brake hand, which is on the same side of the hip the rope crosses. (For example; the right hip to the left shoulder to the right hand.) The rappeller leads with the brake hand down and faces slightly sideways. The foot corresponding to the brake hand precedes the guide hand at all times. The rappeller keeps the guide hand on the rope above him to guide himself—not to brake himself. He must lean out at a sharp angle to the rock. He keeps his legs spread well apart to stay relatively straight for lateral stability, and his back straight to reduce friction. The ACU collar is turned up to prevent rope burns on the neck. Gloves are worn; so is other clothing to pad the shoulders and buttocks. To brake, the rappeller leans back and faces directly toward the rock area so his feet are horizontal to the ground.

Figure 2-6. Body rappel.

Chapter 2

NOTES:

1. Hasty rappels and body rappels are not used on pitches that have overhangs; feet must maintain surface contact.

2. Hasty rappels and body rappels are not belayed from below.

SEAT-HIP RAPPEL

2-29. The seat-hip rappel (Figure 2-7) differs from the body rappel because the friction is absorbed by a carabiner inserted in a sling rope seat that is fastened to the rappeller. This method provides a faster and more frictional descent than other methods. Gloves can be worn to prevent rope burns.

Figure 2-7. Seat-hip rappel.

ALTERNATE METHOD

2-30. An alternate seat-hip rappel technique involves inserting two carabiners opposite and opposed. A locking carabiner is then inserted into the two carabiners with the opening gate on the brake-hand side. Finally, a rope is run through the single carabiner. This helps to keep the rappel rope away from the harness.

2-31. To hook up for the seat-hip method, stand to one side of the rope. If using a right-hand brake, stand to the left of the rappel rope facing the anchor. If using a left-hand brake, stand to the right of the rappel rope. Place the rappel rope(s) into the locking carabiner. Slack is taken between the locking carabiner and anchor point. The slack is then wrapped around the shaft of the locking carabiner and placed into the gate so a round turn is made around the shaft of the locking carabiner (Figure 2-8). Any remaining slack is then pulled toward the uphill anchor point. If a single rope is used, repeat this process to place two round turns around the shaft of the locking carabiner. Face the anchor point and descend, using the upper hand as the guide, and the lower hand as the brake. This method has minimal friction, and is fast and safe. Care should be taken, however, to ensure the rope is hooked correctly into the carabiner to avoid opening the gate with the rope. Loose clothing or equipment around the waist may be accidentally pulled into the locking carabiner and lock (stop) the rappel. For this reason, the rappeller must tuck in his shirt and keep his equipment out of the way during his descent.

Figure 2-8. Proper hookup using carabiner wrap.

FIGURE-EIGHT DESCENDER

2-32. The figure-eight descender puts less kinks in the rope and can be used with one or two ropes (Figure 2-9).
> (1) To use the figure-eight descender, pass a bight through the large eye, and then over the small eye onto the neck. Place the small eye into a locking carabiner. To reduce the amount of friction on the figure-eight, place the original bight into the carabiner and not around the neck of the descender. (Less friction requires more braking force from the rappeller.)

Chapter 2

(2) The guide hand goes on the rope that is running from the anchor. The brake hand goes on the slack rope. The brake is applied by moving the brake hand to the rear or downward.

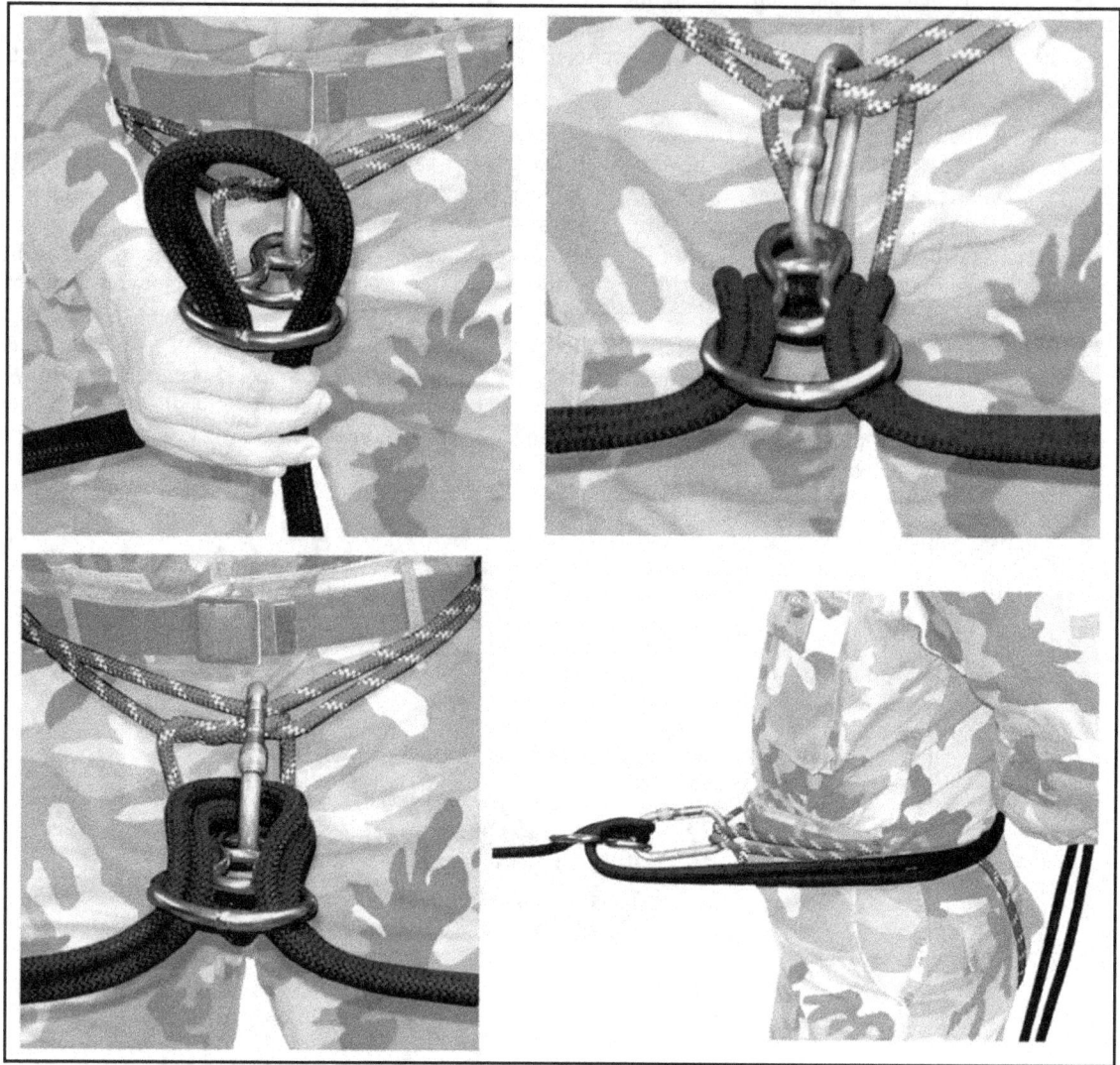

Figure 2-9. Figure-eight descender.

OTHER DEVICES

2-33. Many different types of devices are similar in design and operation to the basic plate. These include slots or plates, and tubers. Most of these devices can accommodate two ropes not greater than 7/16 of an inch in size. Follow manufacturer's directions for using these devices for rappelling.

EXTENDING THE RAPPEL DEVICE

2-34. The rappel device can be extended using either a piece of webbing or cordage to move the device away from the body and the harness, preventing accidental damage. It also allows for easier self-belay.

SELF-BELAY TECHNIQUES

2-35. A friction knot can be used as a belay for a rappeller. The knot acts as the brake hand when the rappeller must work or negotiate an obstacle requiring the use of both hands. The knot acts as a belay if the rappeller loses control of the rope (Figure 2-10).

Ground Rappelling

Figure 2-10. Extended hookup with self-belay.

Chapter 2

BUDDY-EVACUATION RAPPEL

2-36. Use the buddy-evacuation rappel to evacuate an injured Soldier from a cliff or steep terrain. Face the cliff and assume a modified L-shape body position to compensate for the weight of the victim on the back. The victim is top-rope belayed from above, which provides the victim with a point of attachment to a secured rope.

NOTE: To use this rappel, the victim must be conscious.

2-37. The method for securing a victim to a rappeller's back is described below:
(1) To secure the victim to the carrier's back with a rope, the carrier ties a standard rappel seat (brake of choice, depending on the injury) and rests his hands on his knees while the victim straddles his back (Figure 2-11).

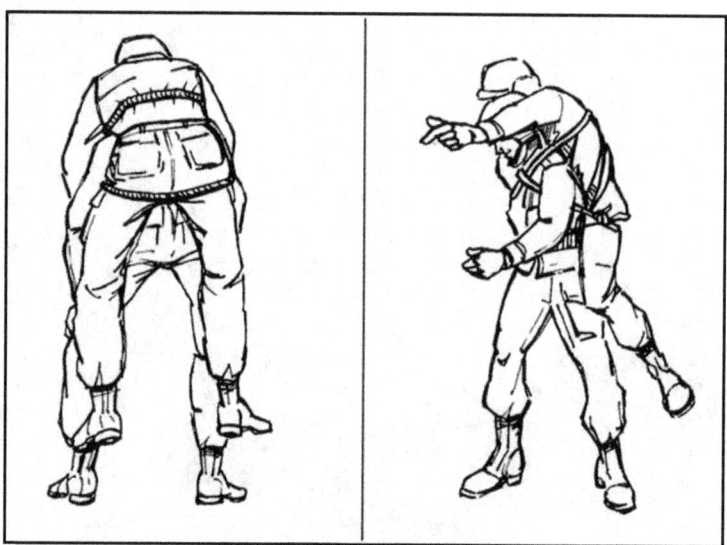

Figure 2-11. Patient secured to carrier's back.

(2) A 4.2-meter (14-foot) sling rope is used. A 45-cm (18-inch) tail of the sling is placed on the victim's left hip. (This method describes the procedure for a seat-hip rappel with right-hand brake.)

(3) The long remaining end of the sling rope is routed under the victim's buttocks and passed over the victim's and carrier's right hip. The rope is run diagonally, from right to left, across the carrier's chest, over his left shoulder, and back under the victim's left armpit.

(4) The rope is then run horizontally, from left to right, across the victim's back. The rope is passed under the victim's right armpit and over the carrier's right shoulder.

(5) The rope is run diagonally, from right to left, across the carrier's chest and back across the carrier's and victim's left hip.

(6) The two rope ends should now meet. The two ends are tied together with a square knot and overhand knots.

(7) The knot is positioned on the victim's left hip. The carrier's shoulders should be padded to prevent cutting by the rope.

ALTERNATE METHOD

2-38. An alternate method is to use two pistol belts hooked together that are draped over the carrier's shoulders. The victim straddles the carrier, and the belay man secures the loose ends of the pistol belts under the victim's buttocks. Slack in the pistol belt's sling should be avoided, since the carrier is most comfortable when the victim rests high on his back.

2-39. A large rucksack can be slit on the sides near the bottom so the victim can step into it. The victim is belayed from the top with the carrier conducting a standard rappel. The carrier wears the rucksack with the victim inside.

> **NOTE:** Rucksacks are not designed to support the weight of a Soldier and his gear. Therefore, this technique is used only as a last resort.

2-40. As described above, a casualty secured to a carrier can be rappelled down a steep cliff using a seat-shoulder or seat-hip rappel. The casualty's and rappeller's shoulders should be padded where the sling rope and rappel lines cross if a seat-shoulder rappel is used. The buddy team should be belayed from above with a bowline tied around the victim's chest under his armpits. The belay rope must run over the rappeller's guide hand shoulder (Figure 2-12).

Figure 2-12. One-man carry.

This page intentionally left blank.

Chapter 3
HELICOPTER RAPPELLING

Helicopter rappelling can provide a means of quick insertion with or without an LZ.

SECTION I — PERSONNEL

3-1. Personnel required for helicopter rappelling include the rappel master, the rappel safety officer, the pilot-in-command, the rappellers, and the belayers.

RAPPEL MASTER

3-2. A qualified rappel master is aboard each aircraft, and safety is his number one priority. The rappel master—
- Ensures internal communication between the pilot and rappel master, and external communication between the aircraft and the ground.
- Inspects all equipment and uses only authorized, serviceable equipment.
- Inspects and tests all anchor points and knots before the mission starts.
- Ensures that all rappellers receive a safety briefing and the pilots and aircrew receive an air mission brief.
- Ensures rappellers are rappel qualified before conducting helicopter rappelling, to include tactical rappelling.
- Maintains communications with the pilot at all times.

RAPPEL SAFETY OFFICER

3-3. The rappel safety officer (RSO) is a SFC or above who is either air assault or ranger qualified. He has overall responsibility for the safety of all rappellers and ensures that all safety precautions are followed. He maintains communications at all times with the pilot and rappel master through FM radio. He alerts the rappel master and pilot of any unsafe acts.

PILOT-IN-COMMAND

3-4. The pilot-in-command (PIC) of the aircraft has the following responsibilities:
- Ensures that the aircrew and all non-aircrew personnel are briefed and understand their responsibilities during rappelling operations, including aircraft safety and action in the event of an emergency.
- Ensures that the donut ring anchoring device assembly and/or aircraft anchor points have been inspected for completeness and functionality, and that they are installed properly.
- Emphasizes procedural techniques for clearing, recovery, and/or jettison of ropes.
- Keeps the aircraft centered over the target with corrections from the rappel master as required.

RAPPELLER

3-5. In addition to the tower qualification requirements outlined in Chapter 1, the individual rappeller must complete advance training under the supervision of a qualified rappel master to participate in tactical helicopter rappelling operations.

3-6. The rappeller must—
- Satisfactorily complete three rappels from a helicopter from a height of 60 feet (two rappels with combat equipment and weapon).
- Demonstrate confidence and proficiency in the techniques, procedures, and equipment used in rappelling from a helicopter.
- Know the rappelling equipment used in helicopter operations and any special equipment required for helicopter rappelling.

BELAYER

3-7. A belayer is assigned to each rope. He is responsible for walking the rope beneath the helicopter during the descent. (Walking the rope is defined as removing the slack from underneath the helicopter by walking backward with the rope as the helicopter descends to land.) The belayer makes sure the ropes are not caught on the aircraft skids or tires to ensure a safe landing.

SECTION II — TRAINING

3-8. Training for helicopter rappelling includes sustainment training and refresher training.

SUSTAINMENT TRAINING

3-9. Before conducting helicopter rappel training, the unit or element conducts sustainment training. Training includes:
- Review of the construction of a rappel seat, equipment to be used, and hook-up procedures.
- Conduct of two rappels on the 34-foot or higher tower wall: one without equipment, one with equipment. Conduct two rappels from the open side of a 34-foot or higher rappel tower.

REFRESHER TRAINING

3-10. Refresher training is routinely conducted to maintain acquired skills. Soldiers who have not performed a helicopter rappel during the past six months will undergo refresher training consisting of three satisfactory rappels from a tower (one with weapon and equipment and one executing a lock-in) before executing a helicopter rappel.

SECTION III — PREOPERATIONAL BRIEFINGS AND SAFETY PROCEDURES

3-11. This section discusses safety, medical and communications requirements, and the procedures to follow during unusual conditions (adverse weather/terrain conditions, night operations). Personnel must use sound judgment to determine what action to take depending on the nature and severity of the conditions.

MEDICAL COVERAGE

3-12. A qualified and equipped medic will be present to respond to any mishap. Medical transportation must also be available. Absence of a medic, medical equipment, or transportation will terminate training. If the situation warrants, and the installation cannot support a MEDEVAC mission, the rappel aircraft may be used as a last resort MEDEVAC vehicle.

COMMUNICATION REQUIREMENTS

3-13. During helicopter rappel training, the RSO will have radio communications with the aircraft. Voice communications are required before starting aircraft rappelling. Additionally, the RSO will inform the PIC to stop operations if an unsafe condition develops.

Helicopter Rappelling

ADVERSE WEATHER/TERRAIN CONDITIONS

3-14. Rappel operations will not be conducted under the following conditions:
- Ambient temperature is 30-degrees Fahrenheit or less.
- Winds in excess of 30 knots.
- Lightning strikes within one nautical mile of rappelling operations.
- Wind chill factors caused by the helicopter's rotor wash or extraction cruise air speeds, which could cause cold weather injuries.
- Water or ice on the rope inhibiting the ability of the rappellers to control their descent.
- The rope is exposed to the elements for a sufficient length of time to freeze, thereby reducing its tensile strength.
- Blowing particles produced by rotor wash causes the aircrew or the rappel master to lose visual contact with the ground.

NIGHT OPERATION REQUIREMENTS

3-15. The following requirements are necessary for night rappelling operations:
- One chemlight will be attached to the end of the rope and one on each rappeller.
- One chemlight will be secured to the attachment point of the rope.
- Night vision goggles (NVG) will not be worn by rappellers during the descent. Aircrew members will wear NVG as required during night operations. NVG lighting criteria will be IAW Army regulations, specific aircraft aircrew training manuals, unit SOPs, or the tactical environment.

SAFETY BRIEFING

3-16. The following safety measures are enforced:
- Loose clothing and equipment are secured.
- Helmets are worn with chin straps fastened.
- Rappellers wear identification tags and earplugs, carry identification cards, and role down their sleeves.
- Weapons are slung diagonally across the back with the muzzle pointing down on the guide hand side.
- All seats and rappelling equipment must be inspected by a rappel master before rappelling.
- No running is allowed within 50 feet of the aircraft.
- Personnel approach and depart the helicopter from the front and forward of the rear of the cargo doors. When approaching or departing the helicopter, personnel bend their bodies forward at the waist to ensure clearance of the rotor blades. At no time will personnel go near the rear of the aircraft.
- Upon boarding the aircraft, the rappeller sits or kneels down, hooks up, and applies his brake hand to the small of his back.
- While in the helicopter, the rappeller maintains eye-to-eye contact with the rappel master and receives commands from him.
- The rappeller ensures that he has a belayer on his rope at all times when conducting training at a hover site.
- During the descent, the rappeller maintains eye-to-ground contact.
- If the rappeller sees his rope coming off the ground or sees that his belayer has lost control of his rope, he immediately brakes and executes a lock-in. He then waits for commands from the rappel master.
- The rappeller brakes once every 30 feet during descent.

Chapter 3

- The belayer does not wear gloves. He keeps both hands on the rope and his eyes on the rappeller at all times.
- All rappelling will be conducted using a double strand of rope.

SECTION IV — DEPLOYMENT OF ROPES

3-17. Deployment of the ropes from a helicopter is a critical task. It can cause a planned rappelling operation to fail, or it can increase the time required to conduct the operation. This is due to the likelihood of the ropes becoming entangled. To prevent this, ropes must be deployed using a positive control technique. Two techniques that may be used are the *deployment bag* technique, and the *log coil* technique.

DEPLOYMENT BAG TECHNIQUE

3-18. The rappeller places the deployment bag (D-bag) (standard) on a flat surface with the stow loop facing upward. If the D-bag still has a static line, the rappeller removes it by cutting the static line where it attaches to the bag. A 12-foot section of the static line can be used as a safety line in the helicopter.

(1) Use a sandbag (about one E-tool spade full of sand) as a weight in the deployment system. Roll the sandbag into a rectangular shape, tie it, then place it in a small plastic bag, rolled and taped. Place a retaining band over the middle of the weight, and place the weight on top of the D-bag. The weight should be about the same width as the D-bag.

(2) Lay out and inspect the two ropes. The working ends (closest to the D-bag) should be even. Place a round turn with the two working ends of the ropes on the weight's retaining band. Working on top of the deployment bag, start forming figure-eights. The stack should consist of 8 to 10 figure-eights, one on top of another—do not exceed the width of the D-bag. Then, starting from either side, center a retaining band over the stack. Ensure that it is over all the figure-eights in the stack. Repeat the process each time, placing one stack in front of the other. Continue until about 10 feet of rope remains. If one rope is shorter than the other, the end of the shorter rope should be about 10 feet from the last stack.

(3) For a primary anchor point, measure down about 4 feet from the end of the shortest rope. Using both ropes, tie a bowline without a half hitch. This knot is the primary anchor point.

(4) For a secondary anchor point, tie an end-of-line bowline with a half hitch toward the end of the ropes. The dressed knot should be 18 to 22 inches from the primary anchor point knot when using the UH-1H helicopter, and 22 to 30 inches when using the UH-60 helicopter. If excess rope remains, S-fold and tape it between the two knots. Ensure that 3 to 6 feet of rope remain from the last stack of figure-eights.

(5) To place the ropes in the D-bag, remove the bag from under the stack of rope. Place the weight into the bottom of the D-bag, and place all the stacks of figure-eights, in the order they were made, one on top of the other into the bag.

(6) Two left, two right, and two rear loops are in the opening of the D-bag. *Do not use the two rear loops.* Close the flap on the D-bag and push the loops through the aligning holes on the flap. Using an 8-inch piece of gutted 550-pound cord, tie the two loops together with a square knot and two hitches. Ensure that two 120-foot ropes are coming out of the center of the flap—not to one side. Repeat the process and tie the right loops together. Wrap the excess rope lengthwise around the bag.

NOTE: The sizes of the loops of the bowline should be no larger than an average size fist.

LOG COIL TECHNIQUE

3-19. The rappeller lays the running end of the double rope along the length of the coiling log (Figure 3-1). He then coils the double rope around both the running end of the rope and the coiling log. The rope must be coiled evenly and tightly.

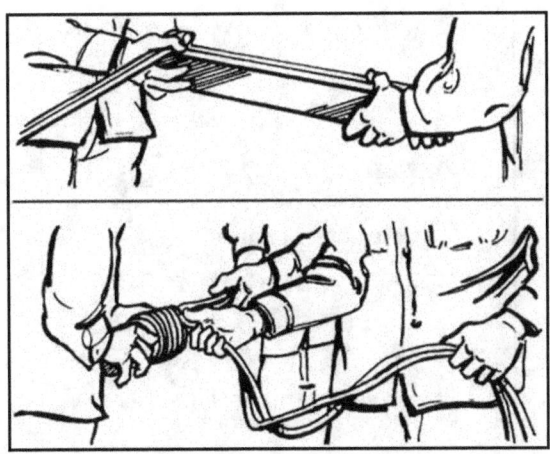

Figure 3-1. Coiling log.

SECTION V — RAPPELLING OPERATIONS FOR THE UH-1H IROQUOIS HELICOPTER

3-20. The UH-1H helicopter provides a safe, stable aerial platform from where rappelling operations can be conducted when landing is not feasible.

CHARACTERISTICS

3-21. The UH-1H is a single-engine, medium-speed, single-main rotor helicopter that can transport eight rappellers, one rappel master, and one three-man crew. It has a lift capacity of 2,300 pounds and is equipped with several floor-mounted tie-down fittings, seven of which are used during rappelling operations.

RIGGING OF THE UH-1H HELICOPTER FOR RAPPELLING

3-22. The rappel master performs the following to rig the UH-1H helicopter:
  (1) Removes all seats.
  (2) Locks the doors in the open position. If no locks are present, removes doors. Also removes small cargo doors.
  (3) Pads and tapes all sharp edges on the floor, door ledge, and all protrusions on the skids. Ensures each door ledge has a scuff pad to protect the rope from contacting the metal door ledge.
  (4) Secures the donut ring to the center of the floor of the helicopter. The donut ring has six snaphooks numbered clockwise, with 12 o'clock being toward the front of the helicopter. The rappel master positions the clamps of the donut ring toward the aft end of the helicopter. He ensures the front two snaplinks and rear two snaplinks are facing outside of the donut ring and hooks them to the tie-down ring with the snaphook facing down. He ensures the center two snaphooks face into the donut ring and are connected to the floor tie-down ring with the gate facing down (Figure 3-2). He attaches the free-floating safety ring to the center floor tie-down ring using a seventh snaphook.

Chapter 3

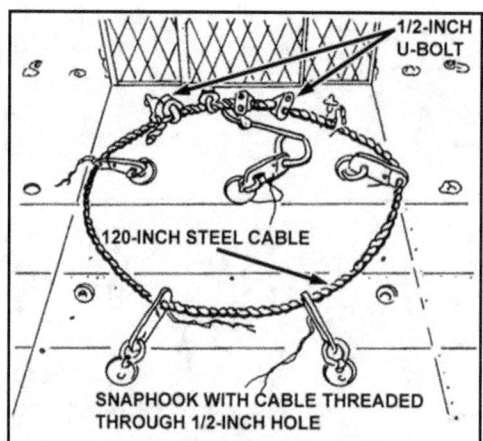

Figure 3-2. Donut ring attached to the floor of the helicopter.

NOTE: Using this technique has caused equipment failure in many aircraft. Therefore, the cable clamp nuts must be inspected and certified as airworthy by the pilot or maintenance crew before flying the mission.

CONSTRUCTION OF ANCHOR POINTS

3-23. In addition to the usual equipment requirements for rappelling operations, an anchor assembly is fabricated. This anchor assembly is commonly known as a *donut ring*. The secondary anchor point is a *floating safety ring*.

DONUT RING

3-24. This primary (or No.1) anchor point for the rappelling ropes is constructed from a 1/2-inch steel cable with a steel wire core. The cable is 120-inches long, consists of 6 strands (18 wires per strand), and has a tensile strength of 21,000 pounds (Figure 3-2). The completed donut ring has a tensile strength of 3,000 pounds. Figure 3-3 shows the donut ring and rappel rope connection in a helicopter.

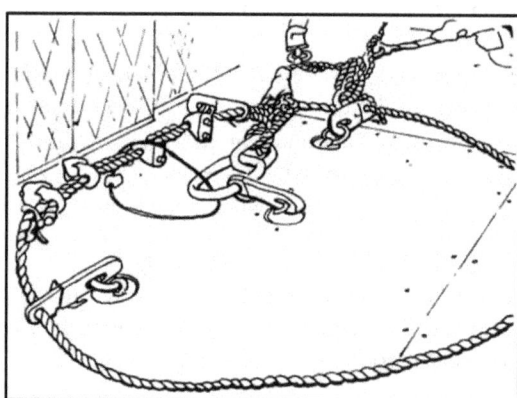

Figure 3-3. Donut ring and rappel rope connection in a helicopter.

(1) Thread six parachute static line snaphooks onto the 120-inch steel cable so four snaphooks are facing out with the gates down, and the center two snaphooks are facing in with the gates down. Drill the end portion of each snaphook to make a 5/8-inch diameter hole, and thread the cable through the holes in the snaphooks.

(2) Overlap the ends of the 120-inch cable 20 inches to form a circle. Secure the ends with four 1/2-inch U-bolts placed at 2- to 3-inch intervals.

(3) Attach two U-bolts to each dead end of the cable so the bolts engage the dead end.
- Before torquing the U-bolts, position a 12-inch length of chain or 1/8-inch diameter cable on the center of the overlapped 120-inch steel cable so it remains in position between the two center U-bolts.
- Tighten each nut of the U-bolts with a torque wrench (if possible) to 40-foot pounds (480-inch pounds).
- After the U-bolt clamps have been attached and tightened, fasten a steel plate (drill to fit) over the open end of the U-bolt studs and spot weld in place to prevent loosening.

FLOATING SAFETY RING

3-25. The floating safety ring is referred to as the secondary (or No.2) anchor point for the rappelling ropes (Figure 3-4). The snaplink at the end of the rappelling rope is hooked to this connection. Either of the following two types of floating safety rings may be used:
- *First method.* Thread an elliptical rappelling ring through the free end of the keeper chain (cable). It is constructed of cold-rolled steel that is 1/4-inch in diameter, with inside dimensions of 2 1/4 inches (minor axis) and 4 inches (major axis). Thread a seventh parachute static line snaphook onto the ring before welding. Weld this ring together so it can withstand a force up to 3,000 pounds.
- *Second method.* Attach two snaplinks to the aircraft tie-down ring in the center of the donut ring. Insert the first snaplink through the free end of the keeper chain (cable) and the tie-down ring with the gate down. Insert the second snaplink through the free end of the keeper chain (cable) and the tie-down ring with the gate up. Tape the snaplink gates closed with masking tape. Then tape the snaplinks together to ensure that the snaplink gates are on opposite sides of each other.

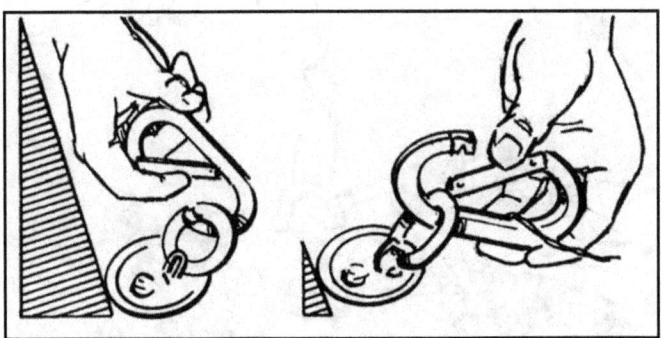

Figure 3-4. Floating safety ring formed with two snaplinks.

RAPPEL ROPE ANCHOR POINTS

3-26. The rappelling rope is connected to the floating safety ring and donut ring as follows:
(1) *Number 1 anchor point (donut ring).* Using a bight about 5 feet from the end of the standing part of the rope, make one turn through the snaplink forming a round turn. The bowline is the preferred method of attaching rappel ropes to snaplinks or anchor systems. The round turn with two half hitches is a reliable means of attaching ropes to anchor systems. Secure the round turn to the snaplink with two half hitches. Make the connection to the donut ring by attaching the snaplink gate upward. Ensure the gate faces upward with the opening away from the knot.

(2) *Number 2 anchor point (floating ring).* Attach the No. 2 snaplink the same as the first with some exceptions. Using a bight about 2 feet from the end of the standing part of the rope, connect the snaplink to the rope the same as the first connection. Tape the end of the standing part of the rope and the knots with masking tape (or green engineer tape) to secure them in place. Make the

connection to the floating safety ring the same as the connection to the donut ring (Figure 3-5). Four ropes can be connected to the floating safety ring using two snaplinks (Figure 3-6).

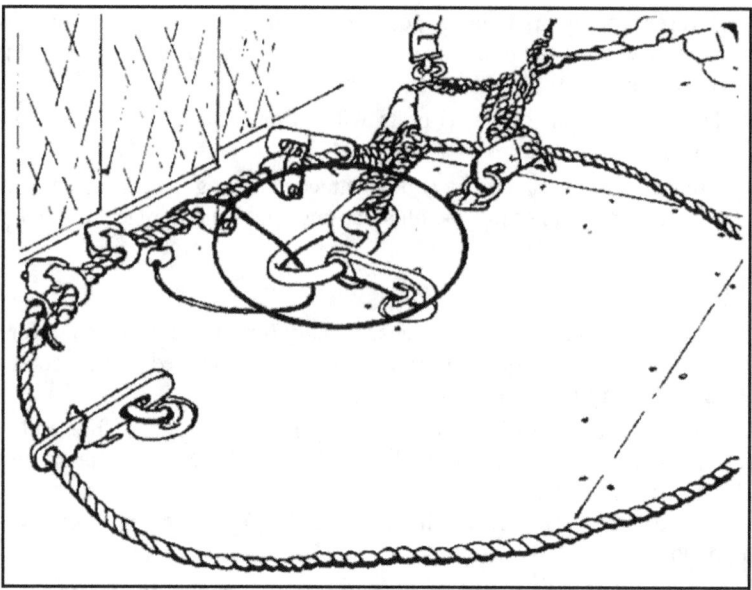

Figure 3-5. Rappel rope connection using two snaplinks for the floating safety ring.

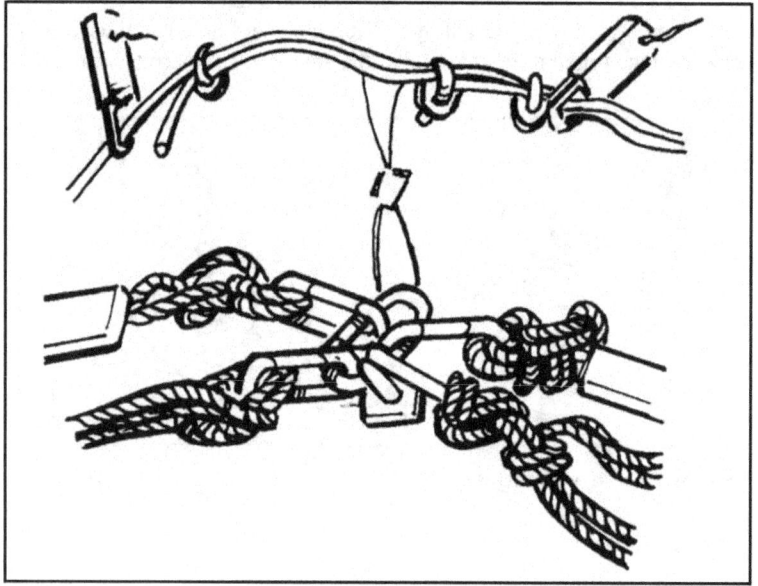

Figure 3-6. Four rappel ropes connected to the floating safety ring (two snaplinks).

SEATING ARRANGEMENTS AND LOADING TECHNIQUES

3-27. Rappelling operations are executed quickly and safely to ensure the success of the operation in a combat or training environment. All rappellers must know the seating arrangements and procedures for loading (Figure 3-7). They must be rehearsed under the supervision of the rappel master before conducting the operation.

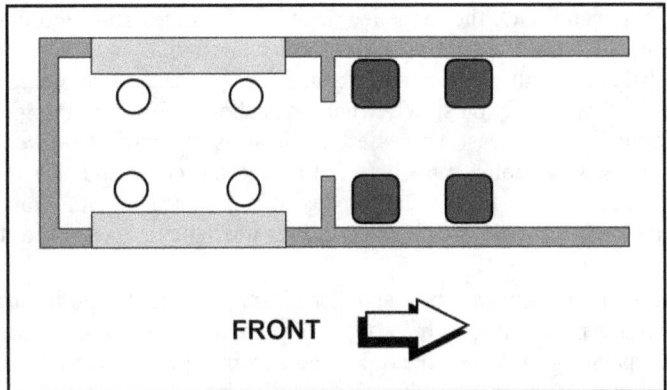

Figure 3-7. UH-1H seating arrangement.

- The first four rappellers are hooked up to the donut ring and use safety belts while in flight. The remaining rappellers use seat belts or safety straps. For safety emphasis during flight, each rappeller's brake hand is in position with no slack in the rope between the brake hand and the donut ring. The rappeller ensures that his rappelling rope is not tangled on any part of the interior of the helicopter or his equipment. He ensures that the coiling log or D-bag is located in such a position that he drops the rope with ease, using his guide hand. The coiling log or D-bag is secured with half of it under the rappeller's inside leg and the other half on top of his outside leg.
- The rappellers should board the aircraft and sit along the leading edge of each door. They hook up with the rappel seat square knot on the inboard side of the aircraft and the brake hand on the outboard side. The rappel master sits in the center to aid visual inspection of personnel and equipment.
- For a flight time of less than five minutes and for training and operations where speed is a factor, the rappel master directs the rappellers to be seated in the door facing outward with their feet on the skid. In a tactical situation and before the helicopter comes to a hover, the rappellers assume an upright position facing inside the helicopter.
- The aircraft is cleared as fast as possible. This reduces the time the aircraft is in the high-hover attitude to a minimum.

RAPPELLING PROCEDURES

3-28. The rappel master ensures all personnel follow the rappelling procedures for the safe and efficient execution of the operation. These procedures are rehearsed under the supervision of the rappel master.

- Rappellers (eight maximum) are identified, and rappel masters tell them which door of the aircraft to exit. Rappellers approach the aircraft once it is firmly on the ground, and the crew chief signals when it is safe to approach. The approach to the aircraft should be about 45-degrees to the nose of the aircraft allowing the pilot to see the rappeller.
- If the rappel master is not already on the aircraft, he boards first and secures himself to the aircraft with a safety harness. He dons a headset to maintain communications with the pilot and positions himself behind the crew chief's chair.
- As the rappellers approach the aircraft, they hand their anchor attaching points (snaplinks connected to their ropes) to the rappel master. The rappel master connects one set of snaplinks to the floating safety ring, and one set of snaplinks (the primary) to the donut ring.
- All rappellers use safety belts. For safety emphasis during flight, each rappeller's brake hand is in position with no slack in the rope between the brake hand and the donut ring. Rappellers ensure that their rappelling ropes are not tangled on any part of the interior of the helicopter or their equipment. They ensure that they can drop their D-bag or log coil using the guide hand. The D-bag or log coil is placed so it does not fall out of the aircraft. Once over the target area, the rappel master issues the rappel commands and ensures the rappel ropes are on the ground (about 20 feet of rope should be on the ground).

- On the command, GO, the rappeller flexes at the knees and vigorously pushes away from the skid gear, allowing the rope to pass through his brake hand and guide hand. The descent is accomplished smoothly at a rate of about 8 feet per second, avoiding jerky stops. The rappeller initiates his braking action slowly when he is about halfway to the ground. The safety officer or NCO ensures that at least a five-second delay is maintained between each rappeller. Another technique used to deploy rappellers is to issue the command GO to the rappellers diagonally opposite each other. In the early phase of performance, the rappeller's feet are together (particularly if over woods or jungle) and his guide hand is used (not the brake hand) to remove any entanglements.
- Upon reaching the ground, the rappeller clears the rappel rope through the snaplink (or rappel ring) until the rope is free. If other rappellers are to follow on the same rope, the rappeller on the ground separates or untwists the ropes and becomes the belayer for each subsequent rappeller. If ropes are to be released from the aircraft following the last rappeller, untwisting and separating the ropes is not necessary. A two-second interval is maintained between exit groups (two men exiting at the same time).
- The rappel master releases the rope from the donut ring after he confirms (by visual inspection) that the rappeller is off rappel. He then drops the rope away from the helicopter.

RAPPELLING COMMANDS

3-29. Helicopter rappelling is conducted in a noise-filled environment. Each rappeller is trained to know the rappel commands and to understand the actions required of him during the execution of each command. Due to the noise created by the helicopter, all rappel commands should be accompanied by arm-and-hand signals. All commands are issued by the rappel master and confirmed orally by the rappellers.

3-30. The helicopter rappelling commands are as follows:

(1) **GET READY.** The rappeller checks his combat equipment, looks toward the donut ring, and pulls the rope to check the anchor point connection. He then checks his snaplink to ensure the rope is properly seated in the snaplink on his rappel seat.

(2) **THROW ROPE.** The rappeller drops his deployment bag out and away from the helicopter with his guide hand. He ensures that the rope does *not* fall between the side of the helicopter and the skid. The rappel master ensures the rope is touching the ground and is free of tangles and knots. The rappeller then replies, ROPE OKAY.

(3) **SIT IN THE DOOR.** The rappeller swings his legs to the outside of the helicopter and takes up a sitting position. (This command applies only to the UH-1H helicopter.)

(4) **POSITION.** The rappeller pivots 180 degrees on the skid. His feet are shoulder-width apart, the balls of his feet are on the skid, his knees are locked, his body is bent forward in an L-shape position, and his brake hand is on his buttock. The rappel master makes a visual inspection of the snaplink and rappel ring.

(5) **GO.** The rappel master points at the rappeller to exit. One rappeller from each side rappels at the same time. The rappel master then gives the command, GO, to the rappellers that are diagonal to each other (for example; the front left rappeller and the rear right rappeller). The rappeller flexes his knees and jumps backward, letting the rope run through the brake hand and guide hand.

ARM AND HAND SIGNALS USED WITH COMMANDS

3-31. The arm-and-hand signals that are used with rappelling commands are as follows:

(1) **GET READY** (Figure 3-8). The rappel master extends both arms to the front with fists clenched and thumbs pointing upward.

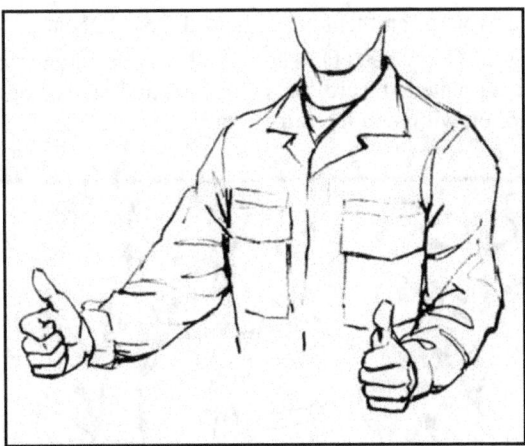

Figure 3-8. Arm-and-hand signal for GET READY.

(2) **SIT IN THE DOOR** (Figure 3-9). The rappel master extends both arms to the front with elbows locked, fingers extended, thumbs running along the index fingers, and palms facing downward. He bends slightly at the waist so the arms are below the waist. He then moves both arms in a crisscross waving motion, alternating left over right, and right over left.

Figure 3-9. Arm-and-hand signal for SIT IN THE DOOR.

(3) **THROW ROPES** (Figure 3-10). The rappel master extends both arms to the front with elbows locked, fist clenched, and index fingers extended. He points at respective rappellers, brings the forearms to an upright position, and then down to the elbow-locked position.

Figure 3-10. Arm-and-hand signal for THROW ROPES.

Chapter 3

(4) **POSITION.** The two arm-and-hand signals for POSITION are:
- **Primary signal** (Figure 3-11). The rappel master extends both arms to the front, elbows bent, forearms pointed upward, fists clinched, and index fingers pointing upward. He makes a circular motion with both forearms rotating in opposite directions.

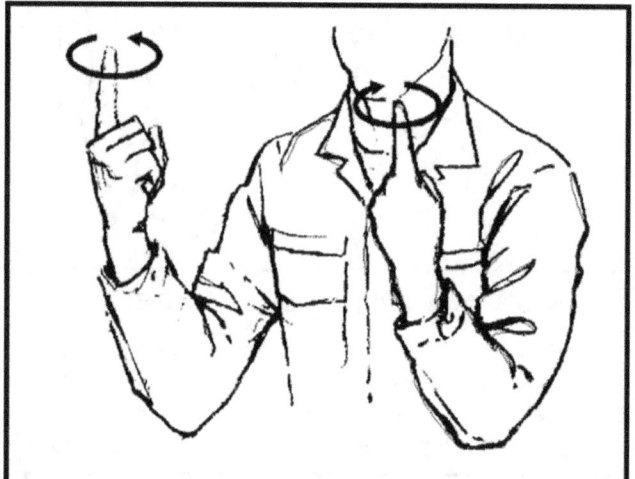

Figure 3-11. Primary arm-and-hand signal for POSITION.

- **Alternate signal** (Figure 3-12). The rappel master extends both arms to the front with elbows locked, fists clenched, and index fingers extended. He bends at the waist so his arms are below his waist and makes a circular motion with arms rotating in opposite directions.

Figure 3-12. Alternate arm-and-hand signal for POSITION.

(5) **GO** (Figure 3-13). The rappel master extends an arm with elbow locked, fingers extended, and thumb along the index finger, and he points directly at the rappeller.

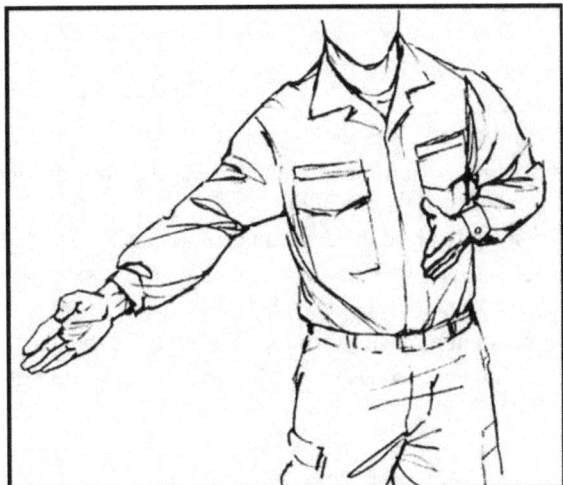

Figure 3-13. Arm-and-hand signal for GO.

INSPECTION AND SAFETY CONSIDERATIONS

3-32. The rappel master and pilot (or his representative) conduct a joint inspection of the aircraft to ensure the safety of all personnel and serviceability of equipment. Inspection should ensure—
- Cargo doors are locked in the open position or cleared for closing, depending on the mission.
- All loose objects in the cargo compartment are removed or secured forward.
- Sharp edges or protrusions on the cargo floor and door ledges are taped.
- The donut ring and floating safety ring are serviceable and properly attached to tie-down fittings.
- A headset and intercom jack for the rappel master are available and operational.
- Serviceable safety harnesses are available for the rappel master and crew chief.
- The recovery rope is installed and properly stowed.
- Unused floor rings are taped down.

SECTION VI — RAPPELLING OPERATIONS FOR THE UH-60 BLACKHAWK HELICOPTER

3-33. The techniques used by the rappeller when rappelling from different aircraft are similar. However, positioning, seating, and the tie-down anchor point are different. Each rappeller is well trained on each aircraft before conducting a rappel.

CHARACTERISTICS

3-34. The UH-60 is a twin-engine, medium-speed, single-main rotor helicopter that can transport 10 rappellers, 1 rappel master, and 1 four-man crew when the center row of troop seats is removed. It is equipped with four 4,000-pound (load limit) cabin ceiling tie-down fittings or rings that are located in the ceiling of the troop/cargo compartment. These fittings are used as the primary rappelling rope anchoring points. The UH-60 is also equipped with eight 3,500-pound (load limit) cargo restraint net rings. Four of the eight rings are located in the ceiling of the troop/cargo compartment. These rings are used as the secondary rappelling rope anchoring points.

RIGGING OF THE UH-60 FOR RAPPELLING

3-35. The rappel master rigs the UH-60 helicopter by performing the following:
   (1) Locks both cargo doors in the open position.

Chapter 3

> **NOTE:** For arctic or other cold-weather operations, or during flights of long duration, the cargo doors are closed and locked until the time specified for opening them.

(2) Removes the center row of troop seats.

(3) Tapes any sharp edges or protrusions on the cargo floor and door ledges that may come in contact with the rappeller or the rappelling rope.

(4) Stows loose equipment forward in the cargo compartment.

(5) Extends the rappel master's intercom cord to the rear over the aft utility drain line and tapes the cord to the overhead troop seat support tube.

(6) Installs the floor restraint provisions for rappellers No.1 through 6.

(7) Rigs and connects rappelling ropes to the aircraft's primary and secondary anchoring points.

PRIMARY ANCHOR POINTS

3-36. The rappel master ties a bowline with a half hitch about 4 feet from the standing end of the rope. He attaches the two primary snaplinks to the respective cabin tie-down fitting ring with gates facing in the opposite directions (Figures 3-14 and 3-16).

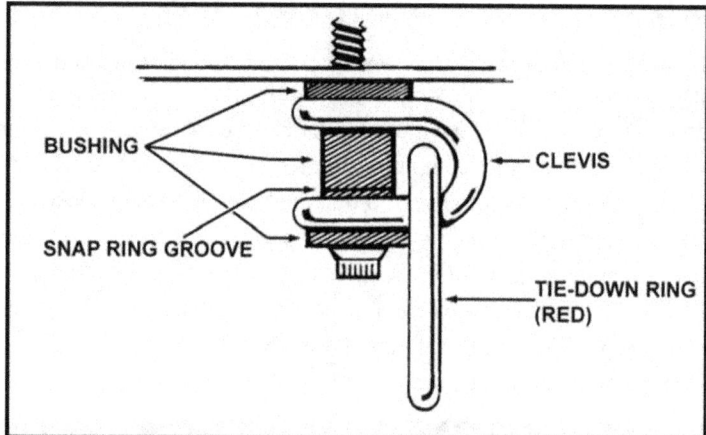

Figure 3-14. Primary snaplink attaching point.

SECONDARY ANCHOR POINT

(1) The rappel master ties a bowline with a half hitch about 1 1/2 feet from the standing end of the rope. He attaches the secondary snaplink to the adjacent overhead cargo restraint net ring (Figures 3-15 and 3-16).

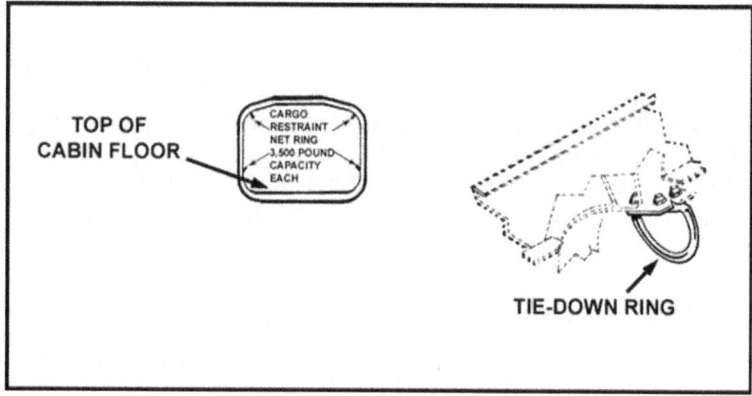

Figure 3-15. Secondary snaplink attaching point.

Helicopter Rappelling

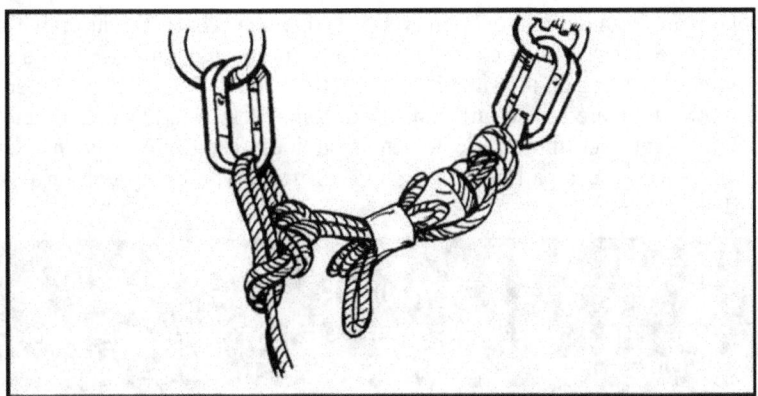

Figure 3-16. Primary and secondary snaplink attaching points.

(2) Removes and secures the cargo hook access door and deploys the cargo hook in the DOWN position.

(3) Installs the recovery rope for endangered rappellers.

(4) Tapes the unused floor rings.

NOTE: There must be a minimum of 22 inches and a maximum of 30 inches between the anchor knots.

SEATING ARRANGEMENTS AND LOADING TECHNIQUES

3-37. Rappelling operations are executed quickly and safely to ensure the success of the operation in a combat or training environment. All rappellers must know the seating arrangements and procedures for loading. They must be rehearsed under the supervision of the rappel master before conducting the operation.

3-38. A maximum of 10 rappellers, with and without combat equipment, and 1 static rappel master is seated and restrained aboard the UH-60 helicopter when the center row of troop seats are removed (Figure 3-17).

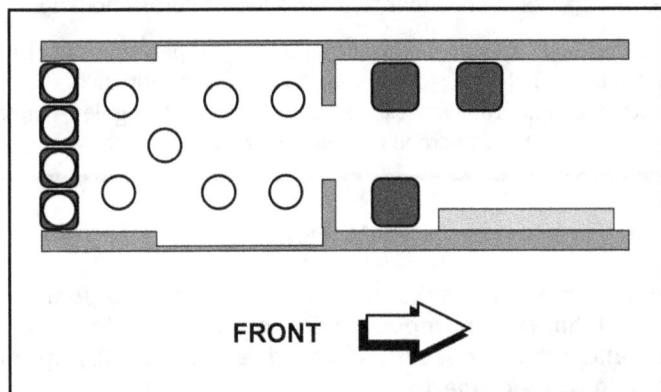

Figure 3-17. UH-60 rappelling personnel seating arrangement.

(1) Rappellers No. 1 through 6 and the rappel master are seated on the cargo floor. The rappellers are restrained using 3 1/2 feet of 1-inch tubular-nylon webbing (or equivalent) that is run through the cargo tie-down rings attached to the floor of the aircraft. The webbing is attached to the rappeller by means of a snaplink that is hooked to a Swiss seat. The rappel master is secured by his safety harness.

(2) Rappellers No. 7 through 10 are seated on the troop seats across the aft end of the cargo compartment. They are secured by the seat belts.

(3) Rappellers are organized into 10-man sticks. They approach the aircraft from the left or right side in reverse order. They are divided into two groups and approach and enter the aircraft at the same time, depending on the situation. Rappellers No. 9, 7, 5, 3, and 1 enter the aircraft through the left door; they are seated and restrained. Rappellers No. 10, 8, 6, 4, and 2 enter the aircraft through the right door; they are seated and restrained. The static rappel master is restrained in the center of the cargo compartment using a C-3A troop-type safety belt or a safety harness during take-off and landing.

> **DANGER**
>
> BECAUSE THE LOWEST ARC OF THE ROTOR BLADE OCCURS AT THE DIRECT FRONT OF THE AIRCRAFT, APPROACHING THE AIRCRAFT AT THIS POINT COULD RESULT IN PERSONNEL INJURY OR DEATH.

RAPPELLING PROCEDURES

3-39. The rappel master ensures all personnel follow the rappelling procedures for the safe and efficient execution of the operation. These procedures are rehearsed under the supervision of the rappel master.

- The rappel master is equipped with a headset and maintains communications with the pilot at all times. He wears a safety harness and stations himself in the center of the cargo floor to maintain control of the rappellers, their ropes, and all anchor attaching points.

NOTE: If all rappellers are rappelling into the same area, individual rappel ropes are not needed. The ropes used by rappellers No. 1 through 4 are used by the succeeding rappellers.

- After all rappellers are in the aircraft, rappellers No. 1 through 4 hand the rappel master their primary and secondary anchor point snaplinks. The rappel master hooks the primary anchor point snaplink into the respective cabin tie-down fittings, and the secondary anchor point snaplink into the respective cargo restraint net rings. After the primary and secondary anchor point snaplinks are secured, the first four rappellers hook onto their respective rappel rope. The rappel master checks the first four rappellers for the correct hookup.
- After the first four rappellers exit and clear their ropes, the rappel master hands the next four rappellers their rappel ropes to hook up. Left-handed rappellers take extra precaution to ensure the correct hookup. Problems can be avoided by placing left-handed rappellers in positions where they initially have the rope to their nonbrake side.

> **WARNING**
>
> Extreme care must be taken when hooking up and positioning personnel that require repositioning of their rope to their proper brake-hand side. Carelessness could result in bodily injury or damage to Army property.

- After checking the rappellers for the correct hookup, the rappel master moves the next four rappellers into position on the floor of the aircraft. After the four rappellers exit and clear their ropes, the rappel master hands the last two rappellers their rappel ropes to hook up.
- After checking the rappellers for correct hookup, the rappel master moves them into position on the floor of the aircraft. After the last rappeller is off the rope, the rappel master releases the ropes.
- If the rappel master rappels, the crew chief is instructed to release or retrieve the ropes.

RAPPELLING COMMANDS

3-40. UH-60 rappelling is conducted similar to UH-1H rappelling, with the exception that the UH-60 has no skids on which to stand. Therefore, the edge of the floor along the door of the helicopter is used as a pivot point to assume the L-shaped rappelling position.

(1) **GET READY.** This alerts the rappeller. The rappeller and rappel master perform final checks of the hookup, rappel seat, snaplink, and equipment.

(2) **THROW ROPES.** The rappeller looks down below the aircraft to ensure that no one is under the aircraft. Keeping his brake hand in the small of his back, he tosses the deployment bag with the ropes *out and away* from the helicopter with his guide hand. The rappeller observes that the ropes are touching the ground and are not knotted or entangled.

(3) **POSITION.** From a kneeling position with the brake hand in the small of the back, the rappeller rotates 90 degrees so he is facing the inside of the aircraft and the rappel master. The rappeller then places his heels on the edge of the floor of the helicopter doorway and leans out into an L-shaped position. His feet are shoulder-width apart, the balls of his feet are on the edge of the helicopter doorway, his knees are locked, and his body is bent at the waist toward the helicopter.

(4) **GO.** The rappel master initiates the rappel with this command. The rappeller flexes his knees and jumps backward. At the same time, the rappeller throws his brake hand out at a 45-degree angle, letting the running ends of the ropes slide through both the brake hand and guide hand.

INSPECTION AND SAFETY CONSIDERATIONS

3-41. The rappel master and pilot (or his representative) conduct a joint inspection of the aircraft to ensure the safety of all personnel and serviceability of equipment. Inspection should ensure—

- Cargo doors are locked in the open position or cleared for closing, depending on the mission.
- All loose objects in the cargo compartment are removed or secured forward.
- Sharp edges or protrusions on the cargo floor and door ledges that may come in contact with the rappeller or his rappelling rope are taped.

NOTE: Do not tape the door latches or handles; this can interfere with door operations.

- Primary and secondary rappelling anchor points are serviceable and securely attached to the aircraft structure.
- A headset/helmet and intercom jack for the rappel master are available and operational, and the intercom extension cord is secured overhead.
- Serviceable safety harnesses are available for the rappel master and crew chief.
- The cabin ceiling tie-downs must have safety wire installed to ensure they do not come undone or unraveled, and the bolt head must be stamped H.

SECTION VII — RAPPELLING OPERATIONS FOR THE MH-53 HELICOPTER

3-42. The MH-53 helicopter is a highly versatile aircraft. It is used for a variety of missions, usually in conjunction with special operations.

CHARACTERISTICS

3-43. The MH-53 is a two-engine, single-rotor, heavy-lift helicopter. It has a crew of six and can be refueled while in flight. Equipped with a precision navigational and communications package, this helicopter is excellent for conducting deep infiltration and exfiltration missions. The MH-53 can fly at night in all weather and terrain conditions. It can follow down to 100 feet and operate from unprepared sites. It is fitted with three gun stations for a mix of 7.62-mm miniguns and caliber .50 machine guns.

RIGGING OF THE MH-53 HELICOPTER FOR RAPPELLING

3-44. When rappelling from the crew entrance door, rappellers connect the ropes with locking snaplinks to the two 10,000-pound tie-down rings under the left scanner's window. When rappelling from the ramp, rappellers connect the ropes with locking snaplinks to the two 10,000-pound tie-down fittings on the left and right sides of the aircraft at station 522. Any sharp edges that could damage the ropes should be padded or taped. A length of fire hose may also be used over the portion of the rope that comes in contacts with the door or ramp edge.

SEATING ARRANGEMENTS AND LOADING TECHNIQUES

3-45. The MH-53 is a large, versatile helicopter. The seating arrangements and loading techniques are numerous. The using unit develops a seating and loading SOP that ensures the safety of all personnel and permits smooth, efficient execution of the mission.

RAPPELLING PROCEDURES

3-46. The rappel master or his assistant are at the two exit points (ramp and door). The rappel master maintains communications with the helicopter commander and relays all commands and time warnings. The commander issues time warnings at 20-minute, 10-minute, 5-minute, and 1-minute intervals. During limited visibility, the rappel master may use NVDs to observe the safety/belayer. Chemlights are attached to the top or bottom of the rappel rope.

NOTE: Night vision goggles cause limited depth perception and a tunnel vision effect.

- The rappel master is secured by a harness and ensures the proper hook up of each rappeller. Once hooked up, the rappellers release their safety belts. At the command of the rappel master, the rappellers position themselves to ease immediate deployment.

> **WARNING**
>
> Before conducting deployments off the ramp, the deploying team members must be briefed on the importance of maintaining separation between members. About 24 to 27 inches are desired. This separation helps maintain aircraft center of gravity limits.

- The rappel master deploys ropes only after the helicopter is in a stable hover over the target area and he has given the command, ROPES. He ensures the ropes are on the ground before giving the command, GO. After the last rappeller is off the rope, the rappel master retrieves or cuts the ropes away.

RAPPELLING COMMANDS

3-47. The helicopter rappelling commands for the MH-53 are as follows:
  (1) **GET READY.** This command is given as the helicopter approaches the rappel site. It alerts the rappellers of the approach to the site and signals them for a final equipment check.
  (2) **POSITION.** This command clears the first rappellers into position for deployment.
  (3) **THROW ROPE.** This command is given once the helicopter reaches a stable hover.
  (4) **GO.** The rappellers exit.

INSPECTION AND SAFETY CONSIDERATIONS

3-48. The rappel master briefs all personnel participating in the operation. He conducts hands-on inspection to ensure the safety of all personnel and serviceability of equipment. Inspection should ensure—
- Tie-down fittings are serviceable.
- All sharp or protruding edges that may come in contact with the rappelling ropes are padded or taped.
- All ropes are retrieved or cut away before forward movement of the helicopter.
- Only three rappellers are deployed at a time; two from the ramp, and one from the personnel door.

This page intentionally left blank.

Chapter 4
EQUIPMENT

This chapter discusses the basic equipment used for rappelling operations (also see Appendix B). It covers rope types, rope selection, and care procedures for each rope type. It also discusses the two methods of coiling, and the different types of snaplinks used to join equipment and ropes.

SECTION I — ROPES

4-1. Ropes are the rappeller's most important items of equipment. They provide access down the obstacle or aerial platform, while ensuring individual safety.

TYPES OF ROPES

ROPE CONSTRUCTION

4-2. Ropes and cord used in mountaineering and rappelling operations today are constructed with the same basic configuration. Construction types follow.

   (1) **Kernmantle Rope.** The construction technique used in this rope is referred to as kernmantle, which is essentially a core of nylon fibers protected by a woven sheath similar to parachute or 550 cord (Figure 4-1). (Kern means core; mantle means sheath.) The internal core of kernmantle rope is constructed of a continuous multifilament-nylon yarn that is spun into continuous parallel strands. This internal core is then covered with a nylon-braided outer sheath.

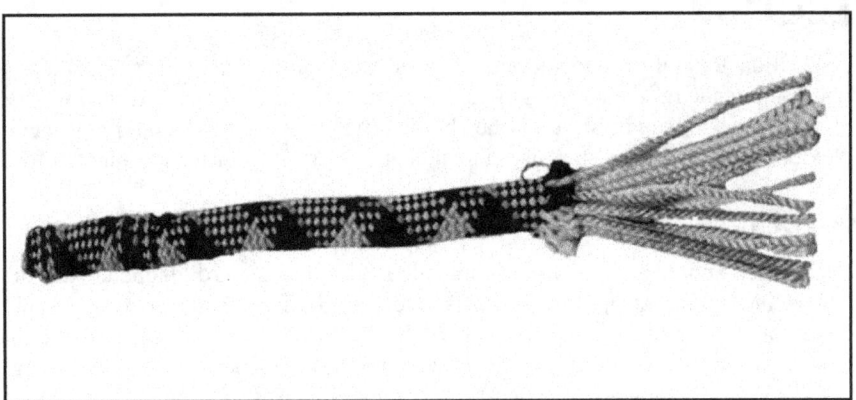

Figure 4-1. Kernmantle rope construction.

   (2) **Laid Rope.** Rope constructed from strands of material that are twisted into a rope of a specific diameter (Figure 4-2) is referred to as laid rope. For years the standard workhorse rope for all mountaineering and rappelling operations was 7/16-inch laid nylon rope. These ropes are easy to inspect for serviceability by twisting the fibers, but tend to untwist slightly when under a load. This untwisting can cause kinking and spinning. Laid rope is also highly susceptible to abrasion. Therefore, laid ropes should only be used for rappelling in extreme emergences. The following specifications pertain to the standard military nylon-laid climbing/rappelling rope:
   - 36 1/2 meters (120 feet) long.
   - 11 millimeters (7/16 inch) wide.

Chapter 4

- At least a 4,500-pound tensile strength.
- Right-hand lay.
- One-third stretch factor (at point of failure).
- May lose as much as 15 percent of rope strength when wet.

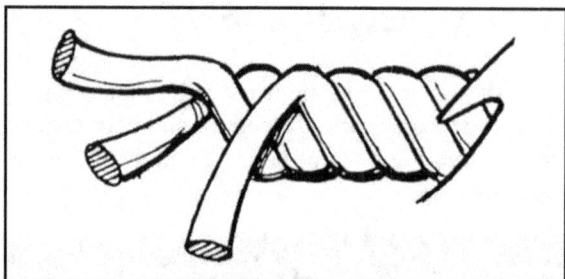

Figure 4-2. Nylon-laid rope.

ROPE TYPES

4-3. Two types of ropes are available to the rappeller today—static and dynamic.

(1) **Static Rope.** Static rope allows for minimal stretch of the rope and is the preferred type of rope for rappelling operations. Static rope stretches about 5 to 15 percent at the point of failure, and about 2 percent under a working load. The minimum tensile strength for an 11-millimeter (7/16-inch) static rope for military use is 4,500 pounds. Static ropes range from 3 to 11 millimeters in diameter.

(2) **Dynamic Rope.** Dynamic rope allows for stretch within the fibers of the rope. This can prove to be a disadvantage in rappelling, Prusik climbing, and other applications. Dynamic ropes are also more susceptible to abrasion and wear. They have about a 5 to 10 percent working stretch. The minimum tensile strength for an 11-millimeter (7/16-inch) rope for military use is 4,500 pounds.

ROPE SELECTION

4-4. Rope selection for military operations requires ropes of various length and diameter types. Rope choice depends on intended use. Selection factors include static or dynamic, environment (water-repellant), climate, and mission (lightweight). Static rope should always be used for rappelling operations because it is smooth, flexible, and strong. It also resists abrasion and cutting, and has a low-impact force.

DIAMETER AND LENGTH

4-5. Rope diameter and length vary with intended use. A standard diameter for many uses is 11 millimeters (7/16 inch). For stirrups, utility ropes, and hauling lines, 7 millimeters (5/16 inch), which can also be used in double strands, is adequate. Standards to remember are; the smaller the diameter, the less the tensile strength; but the larger the diameter, the heavier the rope. Standard rope lengths are 36 1/2 meters (120 feet), 40 meters (135 feet), 45 meters (150 feet), and 50 meters (165 feet). Normally, standard lengths should not be cut. When a mission requires an unusual nonstandard length of rope, the rope should be precut before the mission and clearly marked.

4-6. There are different types of ropes for various uses, so rope should be selected for a specific use. For example:

- Dynamic rope is designed for climbing
- Static rope is designed for rappelling, rescue operations, load hauling, and rope installations.

> **WARNING**
>
> **Using a rope for a task its design is not intended to support can result in personal injury and equipment damage.**

SECTION II — SNAPLINKS

4-7. Snaplinks are used to join equipment, rope, and people into a functioning system. When used properly they are strong, versatile items. Snaplinks are metal (steel, aluminum, or alloys) loops with a hinged, spring-loaded gate on one side. They come in many sizes, shapes, and strengths (with and without locking gates), and in many types of metal. Though the heaviest of available snaplink metals, steel is the strongest.

DESCRIPTION

4-8. Snaplinks are available in many sizes and shapes to suit different needs. A locking snaplink is best for rappelling. Nonlocking snaplinks are easy to operate, but should be used only where they cannot be accidentally opened. Hollow snaplinks should be avoided since their use is limited. The following information applies to all snaplinks:

- The weakest part of a snaplink is the gate. The gate must be closed before applying a load. When the gate is open, snaplinks should have little or no lateral movement of the gate.
- Locking pins should be checked to ensure that they are not loose, worn, or corroded.
- Snaplink metal should be regularly checked for cracks, grooves, burrs, flaws, and rust.
- The spring-loaded gate should automatically close securely from an open to a closed position with no gap between the locking pin and notch.
- If an engraver is used to mark snaplinks, it should be applied only to the gate, never to the load-bearing side.
- A snaplink should never be side-loaded (across the gate) since this reduces the overall strength to the point of gate failure.

TYPES OF SNAPLINKS

4-9. The two types of snaplinks used during military operations are the standard snaplink, and the locking gate snaplink (Figure 4-3). Both snaplinks are available in an oval or D-shaped variation.

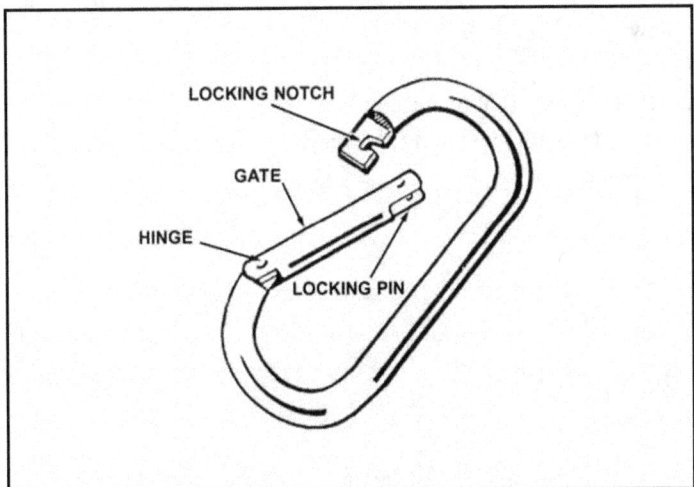

Figure 4-3. Standard snaplink (oval).

D-SHAPED SNAPLINKS

4-10. D-shaped snaplinks are made of steel or aluminum alloys, are available in many sizes and thicknesses, and are designed with or without locking gates. They are stronger than the oval type because the shape directs the largest part of the load to be applied to the longer, stronger side opposite the gate (Figure 4-4). Their strength and durability vary, which must be considered before use.

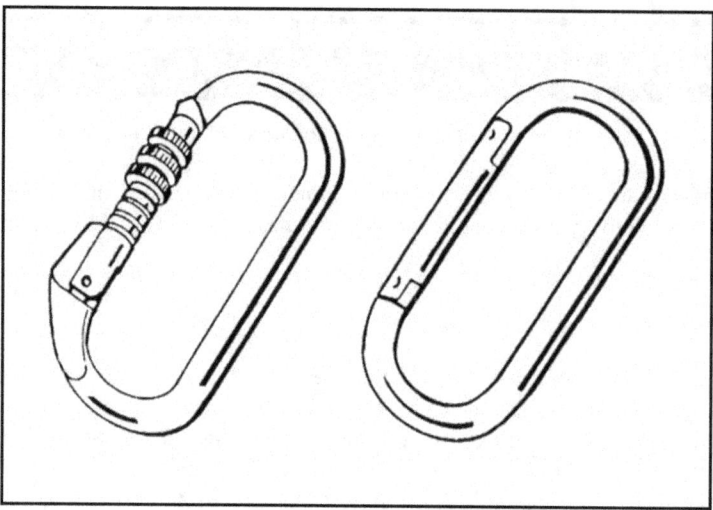

Figure 4-4. D-shaped snaplinks.

OVAL SNAPLINKS

4-11. Oval snaplinks are versatile and have different applications. They are made of steel or aluminum alloys and are available in many sizes and thicknesses. Both sides of an oval snaplink bear the strain equally under load weight. Many modified ovals are available with or without locking gages. All must meet military standards or UIAA specifications.

LOCKING SNAPLINKS

4-12. Locking snaplinks have a locking mechanism with a threaded sleeve on the gate (Figure 4-5). The sleeve screws tightly over the gate opening-end or hinge-end to hold the gate closed. A reverse locking gate is needed to prevent a moving rope from unscrewing the sleeve. The locking sleeve and threads should be kept free of dirt and grit. If the sleeve is forced to close, it may strip the threads. The locking mechanism ages and weakens after repeated use and should be routinely inspected for wear. The characteristics of locking snaplinks follow:
- Material: steel.
- Approximate strength: 2,000 pounds with the gate closed.
- Gate: spring-loaded without locking sleeve.
- Weight: 4.3 ounces.

Equipment

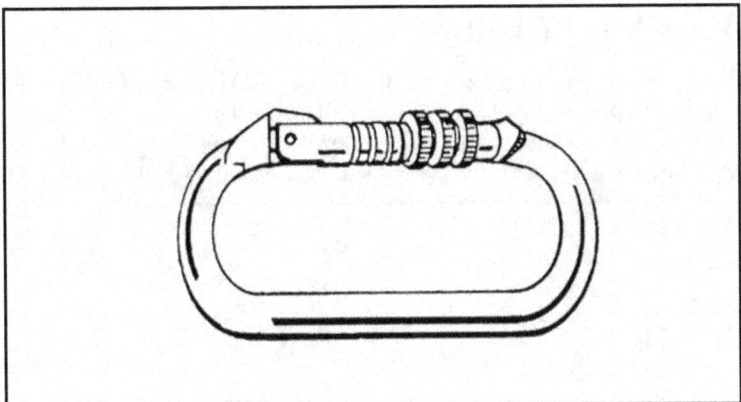

Figure 4-5. Locking snaplink.

INSPECTION

4-13. All rappelling material and individual rappelling equipment must be inspected before conducting a rappelling operation. The rappel master is responsible to ensure the serviceability of rappelling material and individual rappelling equipment.

SNAPLINKS

4-14. Snaplinks should be inspected daily before, during, and after use.

(1) The metal should be checked for cracks, grooves, burrs, rust, and flaws. The gate should open and close freely without binding. There should be no lateral movement when the gate is open. The gate spring action should snap shut when released. The locking notch should have a slant or slot so the gate remains shut under the impact of a rappeller's fall. The gate pins should not work their way out of their holes and should not be shorter than their holes. If there is a locking mechanism, it should be inspected to ensure its threads are not stripped, and that the sleeve tightly locks the gate.

(2) If burrs, grooves, or rough areas are identified, the snaplink should not be used. Rust should be removed with steel wool and the spot rubbed with oil or solvent. The spring should be lubricated as needed. The snaplink must be boiled in water for 20 to 30 seconds to remove the cleaning agents (since solvents and oils cause dirt to cling to the snaplink and rub off on the ropes). It is better to use a dry graphite-based lubricant on snaplinks since such lubricants do not attract dirt.

GLOVES

4-15. The gloves are inspected for serviceability. They are unserviceable if holes are found in the friction-bearing surfaces, or along the seams.

HELMET

4-16. The helmet is inspected for correct assembly and serviceability. A helmet is unserviceable if it cannot be properly assembled, or if any straps are cut or torn one-quarter of their width. Inspection should—

(1) Ensure that the chin strap attaching tabs are secured to the helmet by the locking nuts.
(2) Ensure that the pull-the-dot tab has four plies of nylon and that the chin strap is routed from the inside of the buckle around the horizontal bar and back toward the inside of the buckle.

SECTION III — ALTERNATE METHODS OF DESCENT

4-17. Snaplinks or carabiners that are used for rappelling are placed through the sewn loops of the seat harness or the sewn loops of the seat-chest combination.

FIGURE-EIGHT DESCENDER

4-18. The rappeller attaches a locking carabiner to the harness (Figure 4-6). He routes the rappel rope up through the large hole and places the bight over the collar. He then inserts the figure-eight with the rappel rope attached into the locking carabiner, and locks it down. The rappeller brakes to the rear and descends as in a seat-hip rappel. If heavy loads are to be descended, he uses a double wrap around the collar.

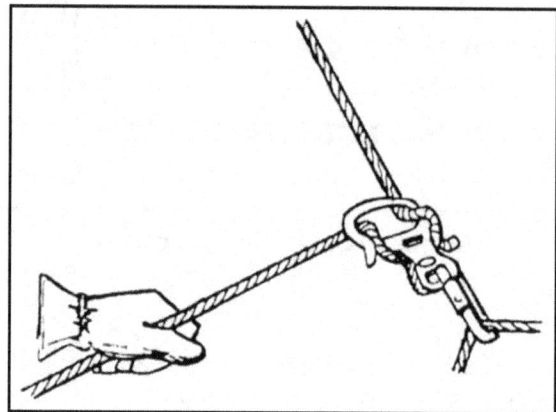

Figure 4-6. Figure-eight descender.

MUNTER HITCH

4-19. The rappeller attaches a large radius snaplink to the harness or rappel seat. He ties a Munter hitch and clip into the snaplink (Figure 4-7). He brakes to the front and descends with an L-shape body position.

NOTES:

1. The guide hand should remain on the standing end of the rope to keep the rappeller's head and face away from the hardware.

2. The Munter hitch creates significant rope-to-rope friction and may cause premature wear on nylon ropes.

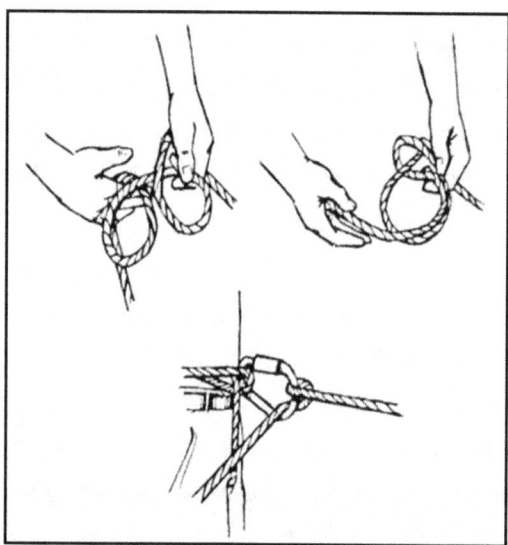

Figure 4-7. Munter hitch.

Chapter 5
ROPE MANAGEMENT AND KNOTS

Serious injury can occur if the rappeller's ropes are not skillfully managed and maintained. Rappellers must therefore be experts in all rope matters. To accommodate this expertise, chapter 5 discusses common rope terminology, management techniques, care and maintenance procedures, and knots.

SECTION I — PREPARATION, CARE AND MAINTENANCE, INSPECTION, TERMINOLOGY

5-1. The service life of a rope depends on its frequency of use, applications (rappelling, climbing, rope installations), speed of descent, surface abrasion, terrain, climate, and quality of maintenance. Constant inspection and maintenance will ensure rappelling rope durability.

NOTE: Any rope can fail under extreme conditions such as shock load, sharp edges, or misuse.

PREPARATION

5-2. The rappel maser must select the proper rope for its intended task according to type, diameter, length, and tensile strength. All ropes must be prepared before departing on a mission—not in the field.

NOTE: For safety and accuracy, ALWAYS avoid rope preparation in the field.

PACKAGING

5-3. New rope comes from the manufacturer in different configurations. It comes boxed on a spool in various lengths or coiled and bound. Precut ropes are usually packaged in protective covers made of plastic or burlap. Do not remove the protective cover until the rope is ready for use.

SECURING THE ENDS OF THE ROPE

5-4. If still on a spool, the rope must be cut to the desired length. All ropes will fray at the ends unless they are bound or seared. Both static and dynamic rope ends are secured in the same manner. The ends must be heated to the melting point so the inner core strands can be attached to the outer sheath. By fusing the two together, the sheath cannot slide backward or forward. Make sure this is done ONLY to the ends of the rope. If the rope is exposed to extreme temperatures, the sheath and inner core could be weakened, reducing overall tensile strength. The ends may also be dipped in enamel or lacquer for further protection.

CARE AND MAINTENANCE

5-5. The rope is a climber's lifeline. Therefore, it must be cared for and used properly. The following general guidelines should be used when handling ropes:

- **Do not step on or drag ropes on the ground unnecessarily.** Small particles of dirt will be ground between the inner strands and slowly cut them.
- **While in use, do not allow the rope to come into contact with sharp edges.** Nylon rope is easily cut, particularly when under tension. If the rope must be used over a sharp edge, pad the edge for protection.
- **Always keep the rope as dry as possible.** If the rope becomes wet, hang it in large loops off the ground and allow it to dry. Never dry a rope with high heat or in direct sunlight.
- **Never leave a rope knotted or tightly stretched for longer than necessary.** Over time it will reduce the strength and life of the rope.

Chapter 5

- **Never allow one rope to continuously rub over or against another.** Allowing rope-on-rope contact with nylon rope is extremely dangerous because heat produced by the friction can cause nylon to melt.
- **Inspect the rope before each use** for frayed or cut spots, mildew or rot, or defects in new rope construction.
- **The ends of the rope should be whipped or melted** to prevent unraveling.
- **Do not splice ropes for use in rappelling.**
- **Do not mark ropes with paints or allow them to come in contact with oils or petroleum products.** Some of these can weaken and deteriorate nylon.
- **Never use a rappelling rope for any purpose except rappelling.**
- **Each rope should have a corresponding rope log** (see DA Form 5752-R, *Rope Log (Usage and History)* or similar type of log. A rope log serves as a safety record. It should annotate use, terrain, weather, application, and condition each time the rope is used (Figure 5-1). DA Form 5752-R (located in the back of this TC) is authorized for local reproduction on 8 1/2- by 11-inch paper.

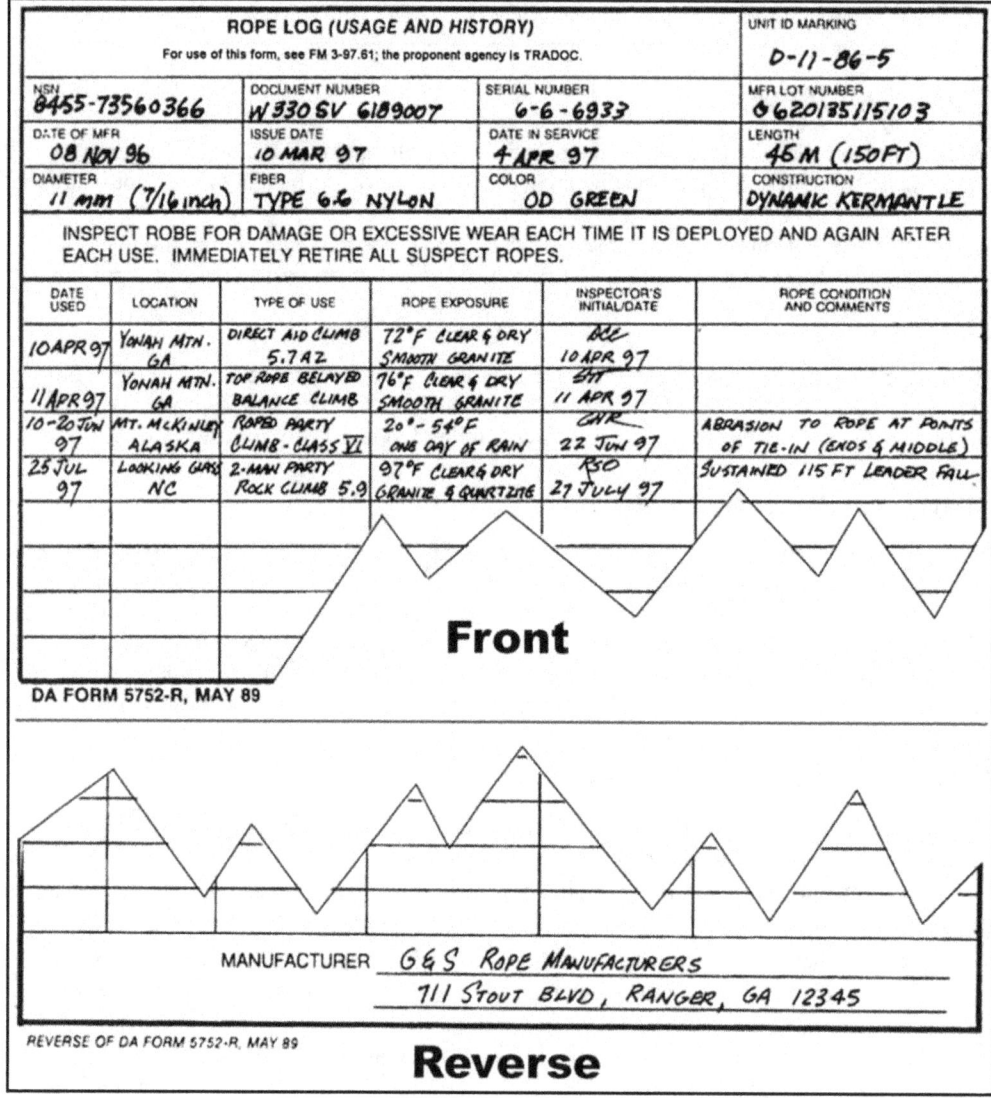

Figure 5-1. Example of completed DA Form 5752-R, Rope Log (Usage and History).

- **Never subject the rope to high heat or flame.** This will significantly weaken it.
- **All ropes should be washed and rinsed periodically to remove dirt and grit.** Commercial rope washers are made from short pieces of modified pipe that connect to any faucet. Pinholes within the pipe force water to circulate around and scrub the rope as it is slowly fed through the washer. Another method is to machine wash on a gentle cycle in cold water with a nylon-safe soap. Never bleach or use harsh cleansers. Ensure that only front loading washing machines are used to wash ropes.
- **When not in use, ropes should be loosely coiled and hung on wooden pegs—not on nails or other metal objects.** Storage areas should be relatively cool with low humidity levels to prevent mildew or rotting. Ropes may also be loosely stacked and placed in rope bags for storage on shelves.
- **Avoid rope storage in direct sunlight,** because ultraviolet radiation will deteriorate nylon over long periods.

INSPECTION

5-6. Ropes should be inspected before and after each use, especially when working around loose rock or sharp edges.

KERNMANTLE ROPE

5-7. Although the core of kernmantle rope cannot be seen, it is possible to damage the core without damaging the sheath. Therefore, check a kernmantle rope by carefully inspecting the sheath before and after use while the rope is being coiled. When coiling, be aware of how the rope feels as it runs through the hands. Immediately note and tie off any lumps or depressions felt.

- Damage to the core of a kernmantle rope usually consists of filaments or yarn breakage that results in a slight retraction. If enough strands rupture, a localized reduction in the diameter of the rope results in a depression that can be felt or even seen.
- Check any other suspected areas further by putting them under tension (the weight of one person standing on a Prusik tensioning system is about maximum). This procedure will emphasize the lump or depression by separating the broken strands and enlarging the dip. If a noticeable difference in diameter is obvious, retire the rope immediately.

TERMINOLOGY

5-8. When using ropes, understanding basic terminology is important. The terms that follow are the most commonly used in rappelling. Figure 5-2 provides visual illustrations for some of these terms.

BIGHT

5-9. A bight of rope is a simple bend of rope in which the rope does not cross itself.

LOOP

5-10. A loop is a bend of a rope in which the rope crosses itself.

HALF HITCH

5-11. A half hitch is a loop that runs around an object in such a manner as to lock or secure itself.

TURN

5-12. A turn wraps around an object, providing 360-degree contact.

Chapter 5

ROUND TURN

5-13. A round turn wraps around an object one and one-half times. It is used to distribute the load over a small diameter anchor (3 inches or less). A round turn may also be used around larger diameter anchors to reduce tension on the knot, or to provide added friction.

RUNNING END

5-14. A running end is the loose or working end of the rope.

STANDING PART

5-15. The standing part is the static, stationary, or nonworking end of the rope.

LAY

5-16. The lay is the direction of twist used in construction of the rope.

PIGTAIL

5-17. The pigtail (tail) is the portion of the rope's running end located between the safety knot and end of the rope.

DRESS

5-18. Dress is the proper arrangement of all knot parts. Removal of unnecessary kinks, twists, and slack to ensure all rope parts of the knot make contact is ensured during the dress arrangement.

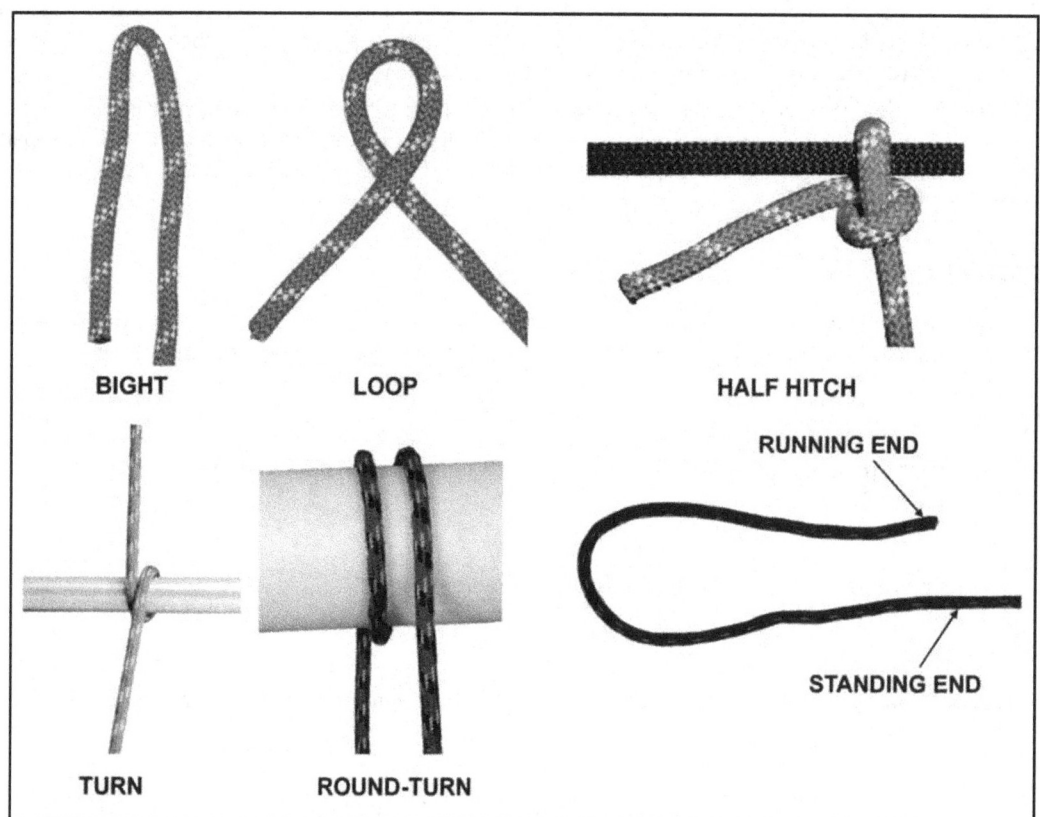

Figure 5-2. Examples of roping terminology.

Rope Management and Knots

SECTION II — COILING, CARRYING, THROWING

5-19. The ease and speed of rope deployment and recovery greatly depends upon technique and practice.

COILING AND CARRYING THE ROPE

5-20. Use the butterfly or mountain coil to prepare and carry the rope. Each coil technique is easy to accomplish and results in a minimal amount of kinks, twists, and knots during deployment.

MOUNTAIN COIL

5-21. To start a mountain coil, grasp the rope approximately 1 meter from the end with one hand. Run the other hand along the rope until both arms are outstretched. Grasping the rope firmly, bring the hands together forming a loop, then lay the loop in the hand closest to the end of the rope. This is repeated forming uniform loops that run in a clockwise direction until the rope is completely coiled. The rope may be given a 1/4 twist as each loop is formed to overcome any tendency to twist or form figure-eights.

(1) In finishing the mountain coil, form a bight approximately 30 centimeters long with the starting end of the rope and lay it along the top of the coil. Uncoil the last loop. Using this length of rope, begin making wraps around the coil and the bight, wrapping toward the closed end of the bight. Make the first wrap bind across itself to lock it into place. Make six to eight wraps to adequately secure the coil, then route the end of the rope through the closed end of the bight. Pull the running end of the bight tight, securing the coil.

(2) The mountain coil may be carried in the pack (by forming a figure-eight), doubling it and placing it under the flap, or by placing it over the shoulder and under the opposite arm, slung across the chest. Figure 5-3 shows the steps involved in routing and wrapping a mountain coil.

Figure 5-3. Mountain coil.

BUTTERFLY COIL

5-22. The butterfly coil is the quickest and easiest technique for coiling (Figure 5-4).

Chapter 5

Figure 5-4. Butterfly coil.

(1) **Coiling.** To start the double butterfly, grasp both ends of the rope and begin back feeding. Find the center of the rope forming a bight. With the bight in the left hand, grasp both ropes and slide the right hand out until there is approximately one arm's length of rope. Place the doubled rope over the head, draping it around the neck and on top of the shoulders. Ensure that it hangs no lower than the waist. With the rest of the doubled rope in front of you, make doubled bights placing them over the head in the same manner as the first bight. Coil alternating from side to side (left to right, right to left) while maintaining equal-length bights. Continue coiling until approximately two arm-lengths of rope remain. Remove the coils from the neck and shoulders carefully and hold the center in one hand. Wrap the two ends around the coils a minimum of three doubled wraps, ensuring that the first wrap locks back on itself.

(2) **Tie-off and carrying.** Take a doubled bight from the loose ends of rope and pass it through the apex of the coils. Pull the loose ends through the doubled bight and dress it down. Place an overhand knot in the loose ends, dressing it down to the apex of the bight securing coils. Ensure the loose ends do not exceed the length of the coils. In this configuration the coiled rope is secure enough for hand carrying or carrying in a rucksack, or for storage. Figure 5-5 shows a butterfly coil tie-off.

Rope Management and Knots

Figure 5-5. Butterfly coil tie-off.

COILING SMALLER DIAMETER ROPE

5-23. Ropes of smaller diameters may be coiled using the butterfly or mountain coil depending on the length of the rope. Pieces 25 feet and shorter (also known as cordage, sling rope, utility cord) may be coiled so they can be hung from the harness. Bring the two ends of the rope together, ensuring no kinks are in the rope. Place the rope ends in the left hand with the two ends facing the body. Coil the doubled rope in a clockwise direction forming 6- to 8-inch coils (coils may be larger depending on the length of rope) until an approximate 12-inch bight is left. Wrap that bight around the coil, ensuring that the first wrap locks on itself. Make three or more wraps. Feed the bight up through the bights formed at the top of the coil. Dress it down tightly. Now the piece of rope may be hung from a carabiner on the harness.

UNCOILING, BACK-FEEDING, AND STACKING

5-24. When the rope is needed for use, it must be uncoiled and stacked on the ground properly to avoid kinks and snarls.

   (1) Untie the tie-off and lay the coil on the ground. Back-feed the rope to minimize kinks and snarls. (This is also useful when the rope is to be moved a short distance and coiling is not desired.) Take one end of the rope in the left hand and run the right hand along the rope until both arms are outstretched. Lay the end of the rope in the left hand on the ground. With the left hand, re-grasp the rope next to the right hand and continue laying the rope on the ground.

Chapter 5

(2) The rope should be laid or stacked in a neat pile on the ground to prevent it from becoming tangled and knotted when throwing the rope or feeding it to a lead climber. This technique can also be started using the right hand.

THROWING THE ROPE

5-25. Before throwing the rope it must be properly managed to prevent it from tangling during deployment. The rope should first be anchored to prevent its loss over the edge when thrown. Several techniques can be used when throwing. Personal preference, situational, and environmental conditions should be taken into consideration when determining which technique is best. Basic techniques follow:

(1) Back-feed and neatly stack the rope into coils beginning with the anchored end of the rope working toward the running end.

(2) Once stacked, make six to eight smaller coils in the left hand. Pick up the rest of the larger coils in the right hand. The arm should be generally straight when throwing.

(3) The rope may be thrown underhanded or overhanded depending on obstacles around the edge of the site. Make a few preliminary swings to ensure a smooth throw. Throw the large coils in the right hand first.

(4) Throw up and out. A slight twist of the wrist so the palm of the hand faces up as the rope is thrown allows the coils to separate easily without tangling. A smooth follow through is essential.

(5) When a slight tug on the left hand is felt, toss the six to eight smaller coils out. This will prevent the ends of the rope from becoming entangled with the rest of the coils as they deploy.

(6) As soon as the rope leaves the hand, the thrower should sound off with the warning, ROPE, to alert anyone below the site.

5-26. The following technique may also be used when throwing rope:

(1) Anchor, back feed, and stack the rope properly as described above.

(2) Take the end of the rope and make six to eight helmet-size coils in the right hand (more may be needed depending on the length of the rope).

(3) Assume a "quarterback" simulated stance.

(4) Aiming just above the horizon, vigorously throw the rope, overhanded, up and out toward the horizon.

NOTE: The rope must be stacked properly to ensure smooth deployment.

5-27. When windy weather conditions prevail, adjustments must be made. When throwing into a strong cross wind, the rope should be angled into the wind so it will land on the desired target. The stronger the wind, the harder the rope must be thrown to compensate.

SECTION III — KNOTS

5-28. All knots used by a rappeller are divided into four classes:
- Class I: Joining knots
- Class II: Anchor knots
- Class III: Middle rope knots
- Class IV: Special knots

5-29. Knot tying is an important skill that can be lost if not used and practiced. There are many knots, bends, bights, and hitches. The following knot classes are provided as a general guide. Some knots may be appropriate in more than one class. With experience and practice knot tying becomes instinctive and helps the rappeller in many situations.

SQUARE KNOT

5-30. The square knot is used to tie the ends of two ropes of equal diameter (Figure 5-6). It is a joining knot.

TYING THE KNOT
STEP 1. Holding one working end in each hand, place the working end in the right hand over the one in the left hand.
STEP 2. Pull the working end under and back over the top of the rope in the left hand.
STEP 3. Place the working end in the left hand over the one in the right hand and repeat STEP 2.
STEP 4. Dress the knot down and secure it with an overhand knot on each side of the square knot.

Figure 5-6. Square knot.

CHECKPOINTS
(1) There are two interlocking bights.
(2) The running end and standing part are on the same side of the bight formed by the other rope.
(3) The running ends are parallel to and on the same side of the standing ends with 4-inch minimum pig tails after the overhand safeties are tied.

Chapter 5

FISHERMAN'S KNOT

5-31. The fisherman's knot is used to tie two ropes of the same or approximately the same diameter (Figure 5-7). It is a joining knot.

TYING THE KNOT

STEP 1. Tie an overhand knot in one end of the rope.
STEP 2. Pass the working end of the other rope through the first overhand knot. Tie an overhand knot around the standing part of the first rope with the working end of the second rope.
STEP 3. Tightly dress down each overhand knot and tightly draw the knots together.

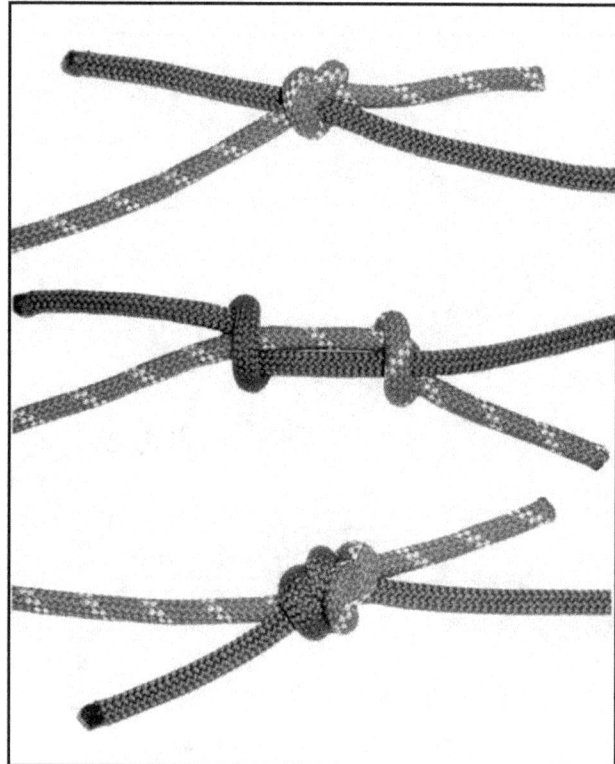

Figure 5-7. Fisherman's knot.

CHECKPOINTS

(1) The two separate overhand knots are tied tightly around the long standing part of the opposing rope.
(2) The two overhand knots are drawn snug.
(3) Ends of rope exit knot opposite each other with 4-inch pigtails.

DOUBLE FISHERMAN'S KNOT

5-32. The double fisherman's knot (also called double english or grapevine) is used to tie two ropes of the same or approximately the same diameter (Figure 5-8). It is a joining knot.

TYING THE KNOT
STEP 1. With the working end of one rope, tie two wraps around the standing part of another rope.
STEP 2. Insert the working end (STEP 1) back through the two wraps and draw it tight.
STEP 3. With the working end of the other rope, which contains the standing part (STEPS 1 and 2), tie two wraps around the standing part of the other rope (the working end in STEP 1). Insert the working end back through the two wraps and draw tight.
STEP 4. Pull on the opposing ends to bring the two knots together.

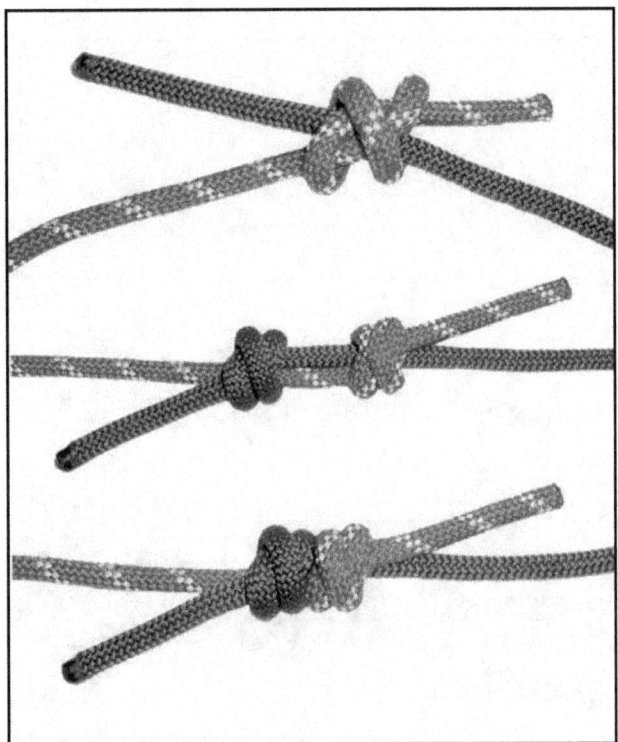

Figure 5-8. Double fisherman's knot.

CHECKPOINTS
(1) Two double overhand knots securing each other as the standing parts of the rope are pulled apart.
(2) Four rope parts on one side of the knot form two "X" patterns. Four rope parts on the other side of the knot are parallel.
(3) Ends of rope exit knot opposite each other with 4-inch pigtails.

Chapter 5

FIGURE-EIGHT BEND

5-33. The figure-eight bend is used to join the ends of two ropes of equal or unequal diameter within a 5-mm difference (Figure 5-9).

TYING THE KNOT

STEP 1. Grasp the top of a 2-foot bight.
STEP 2. With the other hand, grasp the running end (short end) and make a 360-degree turn around the standing end.
STEP 3. Place the running end through the loop just formed creating an in-line figure-eight.
STEP 4. Route the running end of the other rope back through the figure-eight starting from the original rope's running end. Trace the original knot to the standing end.
STEP 5. Remove all unnecessary twists and crossovers. Dress the knot down.

Figure 5-9. Figure-eight bend.

CHECKPOINTS

(1) There is a figure-eight with two ropes running side by side.
(2) The running ends are on opposite sides of the knot.
(3) There is a minimum 4-inch pigtail.

WATER KNOT

5-34. The water knot is used to attach two webbing ends (Figure 5-10). It is also called a ring bend, overhand retrace, or tape knot. It is used in runners and harnesses as a joining knot.

TYING THE KNOT

STEP 1. Tie an overhand knot in one of the ends.
STEP 2. Feed the other end back through the knot, following the path of the first rope in reverse.
STEP 3. Draw tight and pull all of the slack out of the knot. The remaining tails must extend at least 4 inches beyond the knot in both directions.

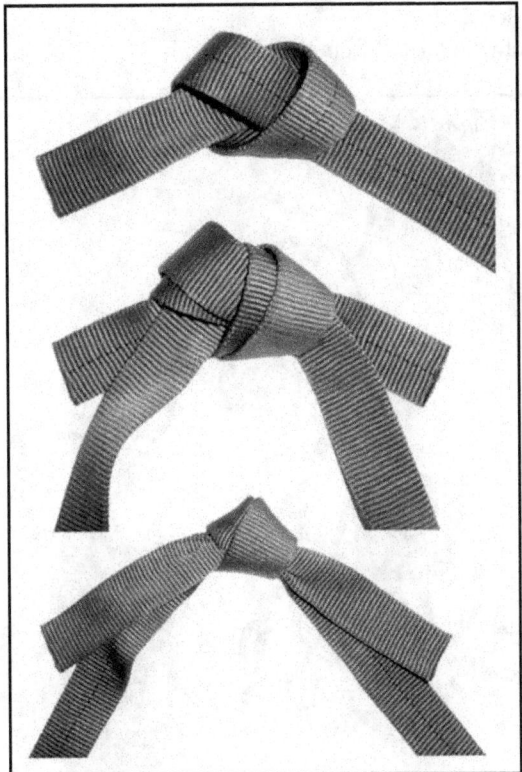

Figure 5-10. Water knot.

CHECKPOINTS

(1) There are two overhand knots, one retracing the other.
(2) There is no slack in the knot, and the working ends come out of the knot in opposite directions.
(3) There is a minimum 4-inch pigtail.

BOWLINE

5-35. The bowline is used to tie the end of a rope around an anchor. It may also be used to tie a single fixed loop in the end of a rope (Figure 5-11). It is an anchor knot.

TYING THE KNOT

STEP 1. Bring the working end of the rope around the anchor, from right to left (as the climber faces the anchor).
STEP 2. Form an overhand loop in the standing part of the rope (on the climber's right) toward the anchor.
STEP 3. Reach through the loop and pull up a bight.
STEP 4. Place the working end of the rope (on the climber's left) through the bight, and bring it back onto itself. Now dress the knot down.
STEP 5. Form an overhand knot with the tail from the bight.

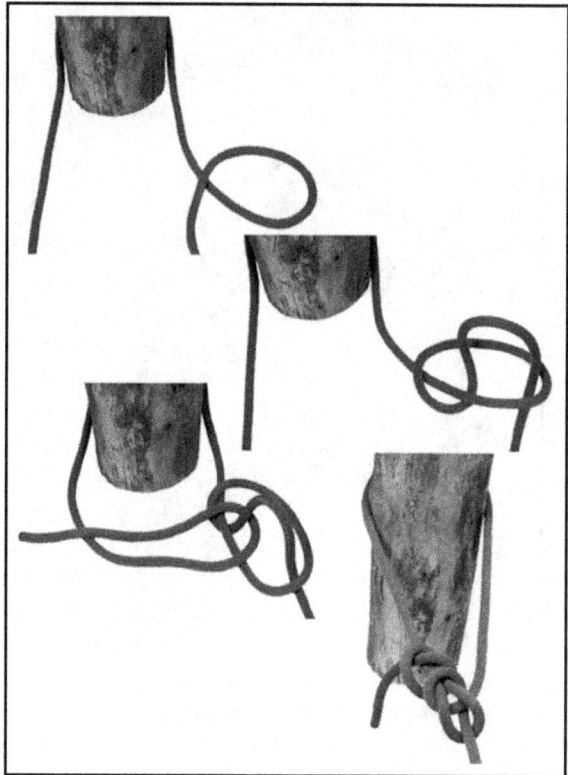

Figure 5-11. Bowline knot.

CHECKPOINTS

(1) The bight is locked into place by a loop.
(2) The short portion of the bight is on the inside and on the loop around the anchor (or inside the fixed loop).
(3) There is a minimum 4-inch pigtail after tying the overhand safety.

ROUND TURN AND TWO HALF HITCHES

5-36. This knot is used to tie the end of a rope to an anchor, so it must have constant tension (Figure 5-12). It is an anchor knot.

TYING THE KNOT

STEP 1. Route the rope around the anchor from right to left and wrap down (must have two wraps in the rear of the anchor, and one in the front). Run the loop around the object to provide 360-degree contact, distributing the load over the anchor.

STEP 2. Bring the working end of the rope left to right and over the standing part, forming a half hitch (first half hitch).

STEP 3. Repeat STEP 2 (last half hitch has a 4 inch pigtail).

STEP 4. Dress the knot down.

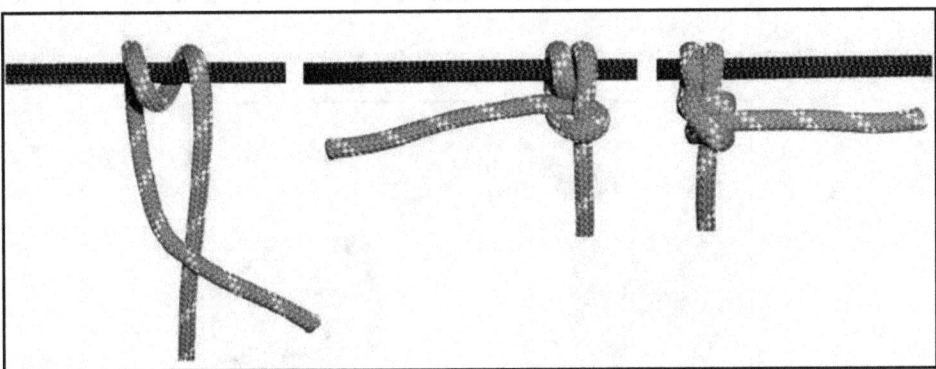

Figure 5-12. Round turn and two half hitches.

CHECKPOINTS

(1) A complete round turn should exist around the anchor with no crosses.

(2) Two half hitches should be held in place by a diagonal locking bar with no less than a 4-inch pigtail remaining.

FIGURE-EIGHT RETRACE (REROUTED FIGURE-EIGHT)

5-37. The figure-eight retrace knot produces the same result as a figure-eight loop. However, by tying the knot in a retrace, it can be used to fasten the rope to trees or to places where the loop cannot be used (Figure 5-13). It is also called a rerouted figure-eight and is an anchor knot.

TYING THE KNOT

STEP 1. Use a length of rope long enough to go around the anchor, leaving enough rope to work with.
STEP 2. Tie a figure-eight knot in the standing part of the rope, leaving enough rope to go around the anchor. To tie a figure-eight knot form a loop in the rope, wrap the working end around the standing part and route the working end through the loop. The finished knot is dressed loosely.
STEP 3. Take the working end around the anchor point.
STEP 4. With the working end, insert the rope back through the loop of the knot in reverse.
STEP 5. Keep the original figure-eight as the outside rope and retrace the knot around the wrap and back to the long-standing part.
STEP 6. Remove all unnecessary twists and crossovers; dress the knot down.

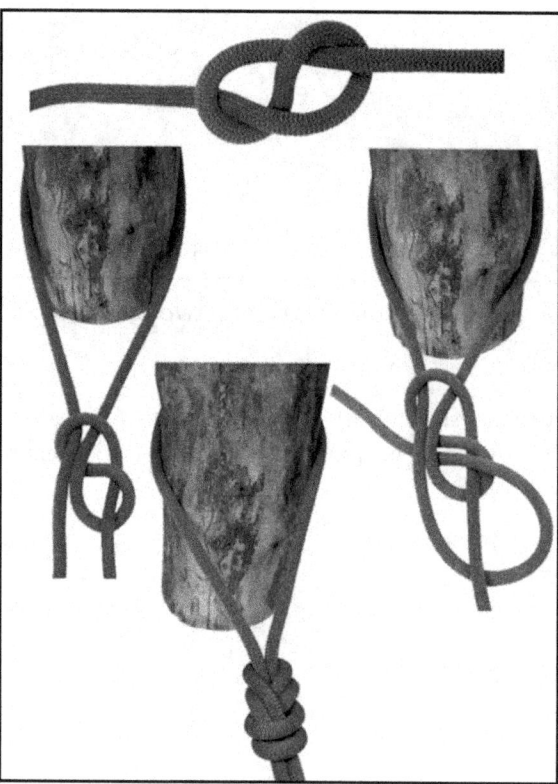

Figure 5-13. Figure-eight retrace (rerouted figure-eight).

CHECKPOINTS

(1) A figure-eight with a doubled rope running side-by-side, forming a fixed loop around a fixed object or harness.
(2) There is a minimum 4-inch pigtail.

CLOVE HITCH

5-38. The clove hitch is an anchor knot that can be used in the middle and end of the rope (Figure 5-14). The knot must have constant tension on it once tied to prevent slipping. It can be used as either an anchor or middle of the rope knot, depending on how it is tied.

TYING THE KNOT

(1) Middle of the Rope.
STEP 1. Hold rope in both hands, palms down with hands together. Slide the left hand to the left from 20 to 25 centimeters.
STEP 2. Form a loop away from and back toward the right.
STEP 3. Slide the right hand from 20 to 25 centimeters to the right. Form a loop inward and back to the left hand.
STEP 4. Place the left loop on top of the right loop. Place both loops over the anchor and pull both ends of the rope in opposite directions. The knot is tied.

NOTE: For instructional purposes, assume that the anchor is horizontal.

(2) End of the Rope.
STEP 1. Place 76 centimeters of rope over the top of the anchor. Hold the standing end in the left hand. With the right hand, reach under the horizontal anchor, grasp the working end, and bring it inward.
STEP 2. Place the working end of the rope over the standing end (to form a loop). Hold the loop in the left hand. Place the working end over the anchor from 20 to 25 centimeters to the left of the loop.
STEP 3. With the right hand, reach down to the left hand side of the loop under the anchor. Grasp the working end of the rope. Bring the working end up and outward.
STEP 4. Dress down the knot.

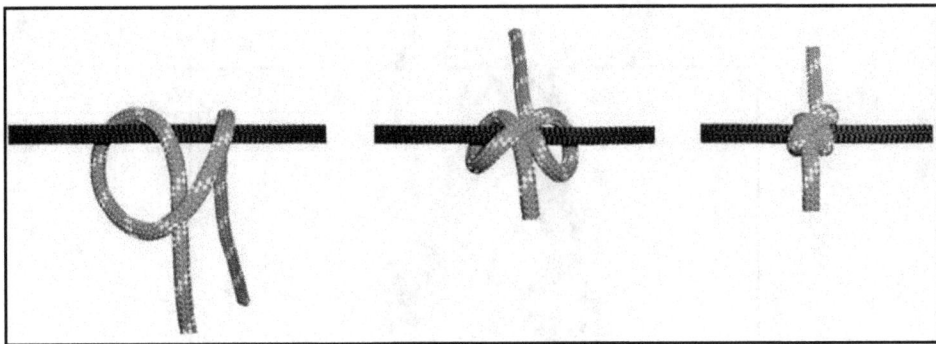

Figure 5-14. Clove hitch.

CHECKPOINTS
(1) The knot has two round turns around the anchor with a diagonal locking bar.
(2) The locking bar is facing 90-degrees from the direction of pull.
(3) The ends exit 180-degrees from each other.
(4) The knot has more than a 4-inch pigtail remaining.

Chapter 5

WIREMAN'S KNOT

5-39. The wireman's knot forms a single, fixed loop in the middle of the rope (Figure 5-15). It is a middle rope knot.

TYING THE KNOT

STEP 1. When tying this knot, face the anchor that the tie-off system will be tied to. Take up the slack from the anchor, and wrap two turns around the left hand (palm up) from left to right.
STEP 2. A loop of 30 centimeters is taken up in the second round turn to create the fixed loop of the knot.
STEP 3. Name the wraps from the palm to the fingertips: heel, palm, and fingertip.
STEP 4. Secure the palm wrap with the right thumb and forefinger and place it over the heel wrap.
STEP 5. Secure the heel wrap and place it over the fingertip wrap.
STEP 6. Secure the fingertip wrap and place it over the palm wrap.
STEP 7. Secure the palm wrap and pull up to form a fixed loop.
STEP 8. Dress the knot down by pulling on the fixed loop and the two working ends.
STEP 9. Pull the working ends apart to finish the knot.

Figure 5-15. Wireman's knot.

CHECKPOINTS

(1) The completed knot should have four separate bights locking down on themselves with the fixed loop exiting from the top of the knot and laying toward the near side anchor point.
(2) Both ends should exit opposite each other without any bends.

BOWLINE-ON-A-BIGHT (TWO-LOOP BOWLINE)

5-40. The bowline-on-a-bight is used to form two fixed loops in the middle of a rope (Figure 5-16). It is a middle rope knot.

TYING THE KNOT

STEP 1. Form a bight in the rope about twice as long as the finished loops will be.
STEP 2. Tie an overhand knot on a bight.
STEP 3. Hold the overhand knot in the left hand so the bight is running down and outward.
STEP 4. Grasp the bight with the right hand and fold it back over the overhand knot so the overhand knot goes through the bight.
STEP 5. From the end (apex) of the bight, follow the bight back to where it forms the cross in the overhand knot. Grasp the two ropes that run down and outward and pull up, forming two loops.
STEP 6. Pull the two ropes out of the overhand knot and dress the knot down.
STEP 7. A final dress is required. Grasp the ends of the two fixed loops and pull, spreading them apart to ensure the loops do not slip.

Figure 5-16. Bowline-on-a-bight.

CHECKPOINTS

(1) There are two fixed loops that will not slip.
(2) There are no twists in the knot.
(3) A double loop is held in place by a bight.

Chapter 5

TWO-LOOP FIGURE-EIGHT

5-41. The two-loop figure-eight is used to form two fixed loops in the middle of a rope (Figure 5-17). It is a middle rope knot.

TYING THE KNOT

STEP 1. Using a doubled rope, form an 18-inch bight in the left hand with the running end facing to the left.
STEP 2. Grasp the bight with the right hand and make a 360-degree turn around the standing end in a counterclockwise direction.
STEP 3. With the working end, form another bight and place that bight through the loop just formed in the left hand.
STEP 4. Hold the bight with the left hand and place the original bight (moving toward the left hand) over the knot.
STEP 5. Dress the knot down.

Figure 5-17. Two-loop figure-eight.

CHECKPOINTS

(1) There is a double figure-eight knot with two loops that share a common locking bar.
(2) The two loops must be adjustable by means of a common locking bar.
(3) The common locking bar is on the bottom of the double figure-eight knot.

FIGURE-EIGHT LOOP (FIGURE-EIGHT-ON-A-BIGHT)

5-42. The figure-eight loop, also called the figure-eight-on-a-bight, is used to form a fixed loop in a rope (Figure 5-18). It is a middle of the rope knot.

TYING THE KNOT
STEP 1. Form a bight in the rope about as large as the diameter of the desired loop.
STEP 2. With the bight as the working end, form a loop in rope (standing part).
STEP 3. Wrap the working end around the standing part 360-degrees and feed the working end through the loop. Dress the knot tightly.

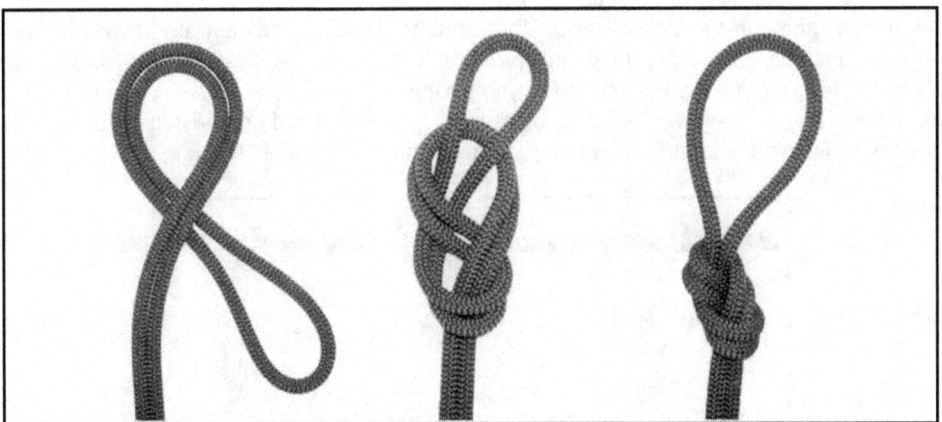

Figure 5-18. Figure-eight loop (figure-eight-on-a-bight).

CHECKPOINTS
(1) The loop is the desired size.
(2) The ropes in the loop are parallel and do not cross over each other.
(3) The knot is tightly dressed.

Chapter 5

PRUSIK KNOT

5-43. The Prusik knot is used to put a moveable rope on a fixed rope such as a Prusik ascent or a tightening system. This knot can be tied as a middle or end of the rope Prusik. It is a specialty knot.

TYING THE KNOT

(1) **Middle-of-the-Rope Prusik knot.** The middle-of-the-rope Prusik knot can be tied with a short rope to a long rope as follows (Figure 5-19).

STEP 1. Double the short rope forming a bight with the working ends even. Lay it over the long rope so the closed end of the bight is 12 inches below the long rope and the remaining part of the rope (working ends) is the closest to the climber; spread the working end apart.

STEP 2. Reach down through the 12-inch bight. Pull up both working ends and lay them over the long rope. Repeat this process making sure the working ends pass in the middle of the first two wraps. Now there are four wraps and a locking bar working across them on the long rope.

STEP 3. Dress the wraps and locking bar down to ensure they are tight and not twisted. Tying an overhand knot with both ropes will prevent the knot from slipping during periods of variable tension.

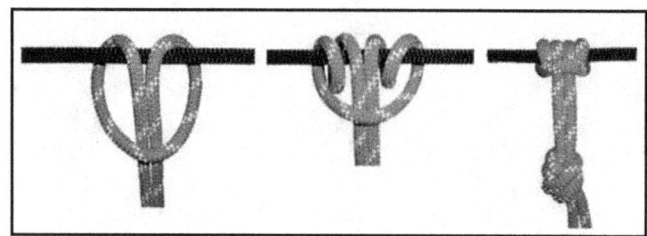

Figure 5-19. Middle-of-the-rope Prusik knot.

(2) **End-of-the-Rope Prusik knot** (Figure 5-20).

STEP 1. Using an arm's length of rope, place it over the long rope.
STEP 2. Form a complete round turn in the rope.
STEP 3. Cross over the standing part of the short rope with the working end of the short rope.
STEP 4. Lay the working end under the long rope.
STEP 5. Form a complete round turn in the rope, working back toward the middle of the knot.
STEP 6. There are four wraps and a locking bar running across them on the long rope. Dress the wraps and locking bar down. Ensure they are tight, parallel, and not twisted.
STEP 7. Finish the knot with a bowline to ensure that the Prusik knot will not slip out during periods of varying tension.

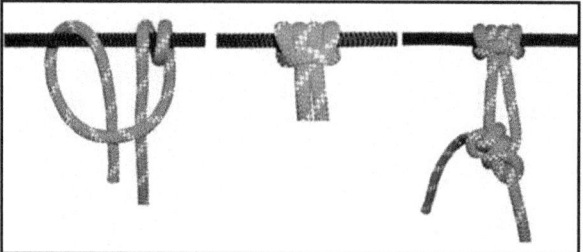

Figure 5-20. End-of-the-rope Prusik knot.

CHECKPOINTS

(1) Four wraps with a locking bar.
(2) The locking bar faces the climber.
(3) The knot is tight and dressed down with no ropes twisted or crossed.
(4) Other than a finger Prusik, the knot should contain an overhand or bowline to prevent slipping.

THREE-LOOP BOWLINE

5-44. The three-loop bowline is used to form three fixed loops in the middle of a rope (Figure 5-21). A specialty knot, it is used in a self-equalizing anchor system.

TYING THE KNOT
STEP 1. Form an approximate 24-inch bight.
STEP 2. With the right thumb facing toward the body, form a doubled loop in the standing part by turning the wrist clockwise. Lay the loops to the right.
STEP 3. With the right hand, reach down through the loops and pull up a doubled bight from the standing part of the rope.
STEP 4. Place the running end (bight) of the rope (on the left) through the doubled bight from left to right and bring it back on itself. Hold the running end loosely and dress the knot down by pulling on the standing parts.
STEP 5. Safety it off with a doubled overhand knot.

Figure 5-21. Three-loop bowline.

CHECKPOINTS
(1) There are two bights held in place by two loops.
(2) The bights form locking bars around the standing parts.
(3) The running end (bight) must be on the inside of the fixed loops.
(4) There is a minimum 4-inch pigtail after the double overhand safety knot is tied.

TRANSPORT KNOT (OVERHAND SLIP KNOT/MULE KNOT)

5-45. The transport knot is used to secure the transport tightening system (Figure 5-22). It is simply an overhand slip knot.

TYING THE KNOT

STEP 1. Pass the running end of the rope around the anchor point passing it back under the standing portion (leading to the far side anchor) forming a loop.

STEP 2. Form a bight with the running end of the rope. Pass over the standing portion down through the loop and dress it down toward the anchor point.

STEP 3. Secure the knot by tying a half hitch around the standing portion with the bight.

Figure 5-22. Transport knot (overhand slip knot/mule knot).

KLEIMHIEST KNOT

5-46. The Kleimhiest knot provides a moveable, easily adjustable, high-tension knot capable of holding extremely heavy loads while being pulled tight (Figure 5-23). It is a special-purpose knot.

TYING THE KNOT

STEP 1. Using a utility rope or webbing, offset the ends by 12 inches. With the ends offset, find the center of the rope and form a bight. Lay the bight over a horizontal rope.
STEP 2. Wrap the tails of the utility rope around the horizontal rope back toward the direction of pull. Wrap at least four complete turns.
STEP 3. With the remaining tails of the utility rope, pass them through the bight (see STEP 1).
STEP 4. Join the two ends of the tail with a joining knot.
STEP 5. Dress the knot down tightly so all wraps are touching.

NOTE: Spectra should not be used for the Kleimhiest knot. It has a low melting point and tends to slip.

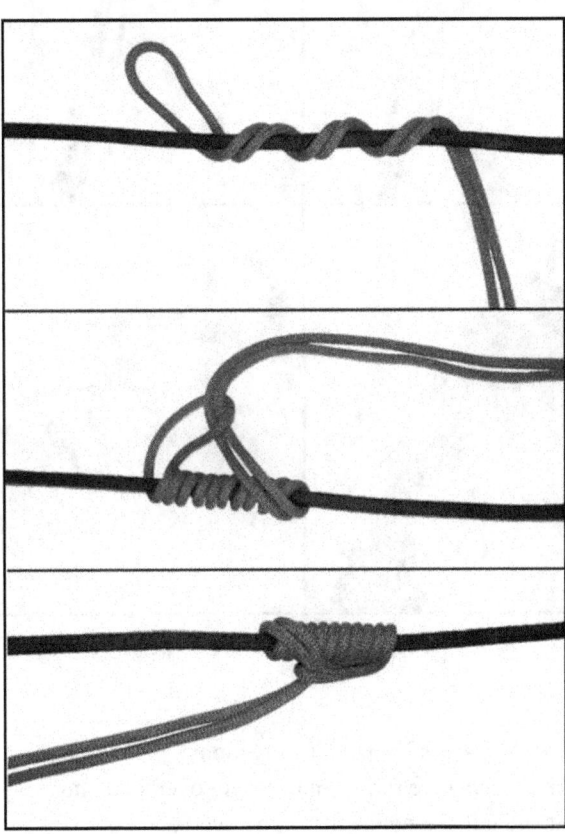

Figure 5-23. Kleimhiest knot.

CHECKPOINTS

(1) The bight is opposite the direction of pull.
(2) All wraps are tight and touching.
(3) The ends of the utility rope are properly secured with a joining knot.

Chapter 5

FROST KNOT

5-47. The frost knot is used when working with webbing (Figure 5-24). Used to create the top loop of an etrier, it is a special-purpose knot.

TYING THE KNOT
STEP 1. Lap one end (a bight) of webbing over the other about 10 to 12 inches.
STEP 2. Tie an overhand knot with the newly formed triple-strand webbing; dress tightly.

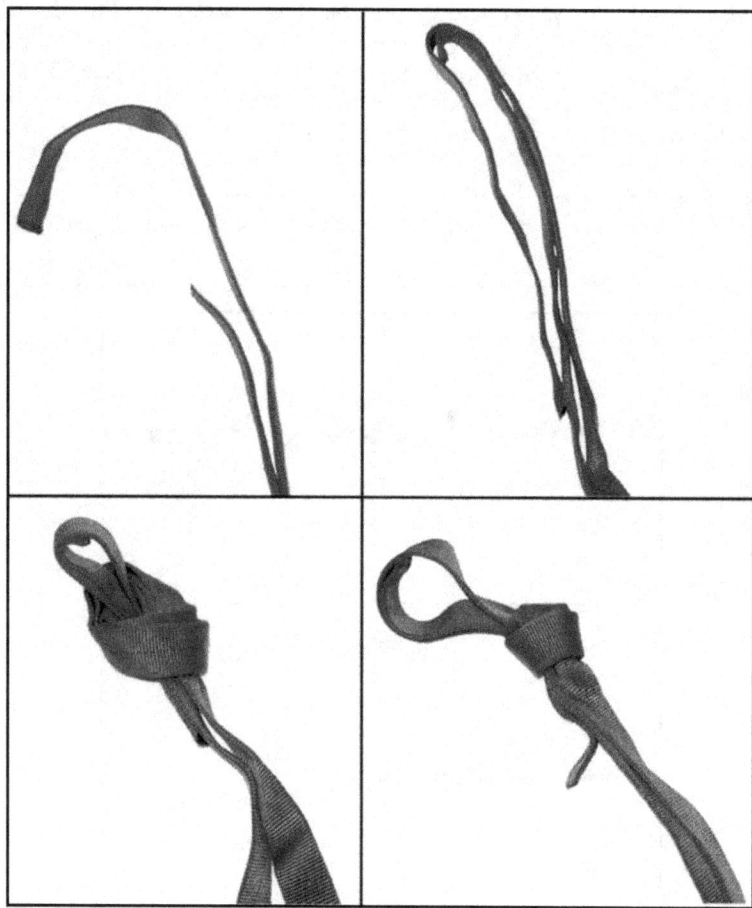

Figure 5-24. Frost knot.

CHECKPOINTS
(1) The tails of the webbing run in opposite directions.
(2) Three strands of webbing are formed into a tight overhand knot.
(3) There is a bight and tail exiting the top of the overhand knot.

GIRTH HITCH

5-48. The girth hitch is used to attach a runner to an anchor or piece of equipment (Figure 5-25). It is a special-purpose knot.

TYING THE KNOT
STEP 1. Form a bight.
STEP 2. Bring the runner back through the bight.
STEP 3. Cinch the knot tightly.

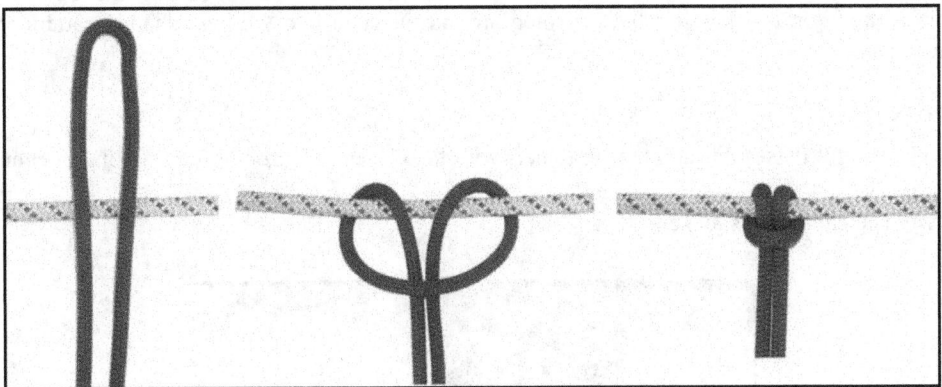

Figure 5-25. Girth hitch.

CHECKPOINT
(1) Two wraps exist with a locking bar running across the wraps.

(2) The knot is dressed tightly.

Chapter 5

MUNTER HITCH

5-49. When used in conjunction with a pear-shaped locking carabiner, the Munter hitch is used to form a mechanical belay (Figure 5-26).

TYING THE KNOT
STEP 1. Hold the rope in both hands, palms down about 12 inches apart.
STEP 2. With the right hand, form a loop away from the body toward the left hand. Hold the loop with the left hand.
STEP 3. With the right hand, place the rope that comes from the bottom of the loop over the top of the loop.
STEP 4. Place the bight that has just been formed around the rope into the pear shaped carabiner. Lock the locking mechanism.

CHECK POINTS
(1) A bight passes through the carabiner, with the closed end around the standing or running part of the rope.
(2) The carabiner is locked.

Figure 5-26. Munter hitch.

RAPPEL SEAT

5-50. The rappel seat is an improvised seat rappel harness made of rope (Figure 5-27). It usually requires a sling rope 14 feet or longer.

TYING THE KNOT

STEP 1. Find the middle of the sling rope and make a bight.
STEP 2. Decide which hand will be used as the brake hand and place the bight on the opposite hip.
STEP 3. Reach around behind and grab a single strand of rope. Bring it around the waist to the front and tie two overhands on the other strand of rope. This creates a loop around the waist.
STEP 4. Pass the two ends between the legs, ensuring they do not cross.
STEP 5. Pass the two ends up under the loop around the waist, bisecting the pocket flaps on the trousers. Pull up on the ropes, tightening the seat.
STEP 6. From rear to front, pass the two ends through the leg loops creating a half hitch on both hips.
STEP 7. Bring the longer of the two ends across the front to the nonbrake hand hip and secure the two ends with a square knot safetied with overhand knots. Tuck any excess rope in the pocket below the square knot.

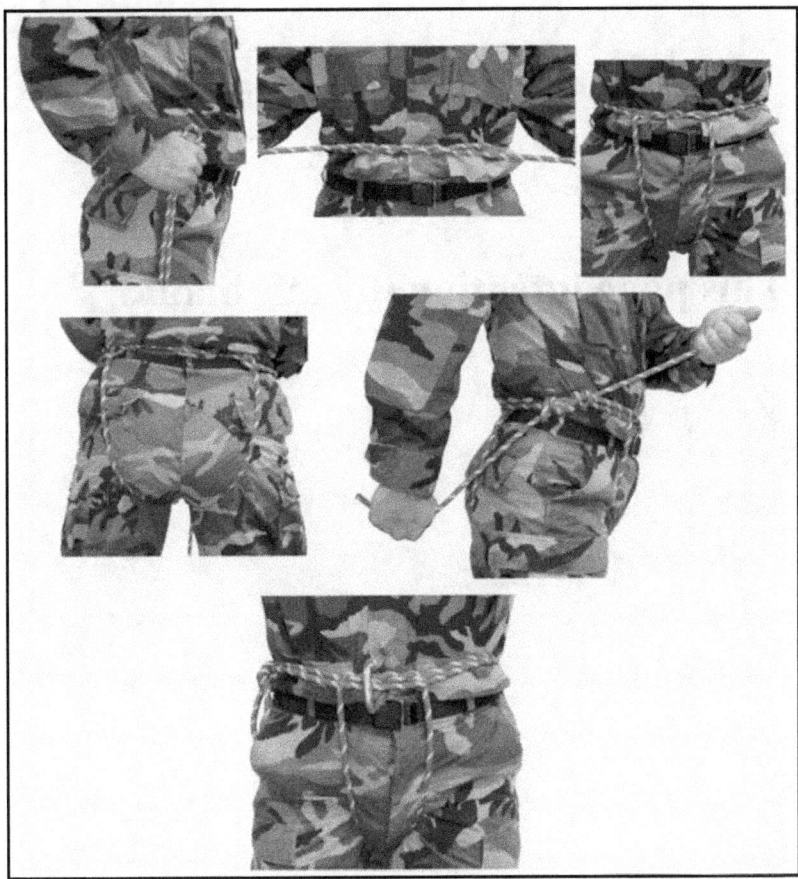

Figure 5-27. Rappel seat.

CHECK POINTS

(1) There are two overhand knots in the front.
(2) The ropes are not crossed between the legs.
(3) A half hitch is formed on each hip.
(4) Seat is secured with a square knot with overhand safeties on the non-brake hand side.
(5) There is a minimum 4-inch pigtail after the overhand safeties are tied.

This page intentionally left blank.

Appendix A
RISK ASSESSMENT

This appendix explains risk assessment for rappel operations. A risk assessment matrix is shown in Table A-1. Reference FM 5-19, *Composite Risk Management*, for in-depth instruction on identifying and managing operational risks.

EFFECT

(1) **Catastrophic.** Death or permanent total disability, system loss, major property damage.

(2) **Critical.** Permanent partial disability, temporary total disability in excess of three months, major system damage, significant property damage.

(3) **Moderate.** Minor injury, lost workday accident, compensable injury or illness, minor system damage, minor property damage.

(4) **Negligible.** First aid or minor supportive medical treatment, minor system impairment.

PROBABILITY

FREQUENT

(1) Individual Soldier or item: Occurs often in career or equipment service life.

(2) All Soldiers exposed or item inventory: Continuously experienced.

LIKELY

(1) Individual Soldier or item: Occurs several times in career or equipment service life.

(2) All Soldiers exposed or item inventory: Occurs frequently.

OCCASIONAL

(1) Individual Soldier or item: Occurs sometime in career or equipment service life.

(2) All Soldiers exposed or item inventory: Occurs sporadically, or several times during inventory service life.

SELDOM

(1) Individual Soldier or item: Possible to occur in career or equipment service life.

(2) All Soldiers exposed or item inventory: Remote chance of occurrence; expected to occur sometime during inventory service life.

UNLIKELY

(1) Individual Soldier or item: Can assume will not occur during career or equipment service life.

(2) All Soldiers exposed or item inventory: Possible, but improbable; occurs only very rarely.

RISK LEVELS

(1) **Extremely High.** Loss of ability to accomplish mission.
(2) **High.** Significantly degrades mission capabilities in terms of required mission standards.
(3) **Medium.** Degrades mission capabilities in terms of required mission standards.
(4) **Low.** Little or no impact on mission accomplishment.

Table A-1. Risk assessment matrix.

RISK ASSESSMENT		HAZARD PROBABILITY				
		Frequent A	Likely B	Occasional C	Seldom D	Unlikely E
E F F E C T	Catastrophic I	Extremely High	Extremely High	High	High	Medium
	Critical II	Extremely High	High	High	Medium	Low
	Moderate III	High	Medium	Medium	Low	Low
	Negligible IV	Medium	Low	Low	Low	Low

Appendix B
BASIC EQUIPMENT FOR RAPPEL OPERATIONS

The equipment listed in this appendix comprise the standard basic items required to conduct ground and air rappelling operations.

GROUND OPERATIONS

B-1. For ground operations, the following equipment is needed:
- Nylon rope, 120 feet (NSN 4020-00-931-8793).
- Snaplinks (NSN 8465-00-360-0228).
- Gloves (NSN 8415-00-268-7868).
- Rope coiling log or standard deployment bag.
- Rappel seat.
- Rappel rings (used as expedient anchor points).

AIR OPERATIONS

B-2. For air operations, the following equipment is needed:
- All items in paragraph B-1.
- Donut ring (UH-1H operations only) (locally produced TSC item).
- Safety floating ring.
- Two 6-foot safety ropes (with snaplinks).
- Eight 120-foot nylon ropes.
- Monkey harness for static rappel master.
- Sixteen snaplinks (UH-60 operations).
- Twenty-two snaplinks (UH-1H operations).
- FM communications.
- Aircraft communications headset.

This page intentionally left blank.

GLOSSARY

ACRONYMS AND ABBREVATIONS

Acronym/Term	Definition
AFR	assistant fast-rope master
AGL	above ground level
AMC	air mission commander
ATP	aircrew training program
CGU	modified helicopter safety strap
cm	centimeter
D-bag	deployment bag
FRM	fast-rope master
GSO	ground safety officer
LBE	load-bearing equipment
LBV	load-bearing vest
LZ	landing zone
MSO	mountaineering safety officer
NSN	national stock number
NVG	night vision goggles
PIC	pilot-in-command
RATELO	radiotelephone operator
RSO	rappel safety officer
STABO	system for extracting personnel by helicopter (combined first surname letters of five system designers)
SSO	STABO system operator
UIAA	Union of International Alpine Association
UH	utility helicopter

This page intentionally left blank.

References

DOCUMENTS NEEDED

This document must be available to the intended users of this publication.

FM 5-19, *Composite Risk Management*. 21 August 2006.

RECOMMENDED READING

The following sources contain relevant supplemental information.

FM 3-21.38, *Pathfinder Operations*. 25 April 2006.

FM 7-93, *Long-Range Surveillance Unit Operations*. 03 October 1995.

FM 3-97.61, *Military Mountaineering*. 26 August 2002.

FM 3-21.220 (57-220), *Static Line Parachuting Techniques and Training*. 23 September 2003.

TM 10-1670-262-12&P, Operator and Unit Maintenance Manual Including Repair Parts and Special Tools List Personnel Insertion/Extraction Systems for STABO (NSN 1670-00-168-5952) (1670-00-6064) (1670-00-168-6063) Fast Rope Insertion/Extraction System (4020-01-338-3307) (4020-01-338-3308) (4020-01-338-3309) and Anchoring Device (1670-00-999-3544). 25 September 1992.

USASOC Regulation 350-2, *Training Airborne Operations*. 27 September 2001.

USSOCOM Regulation 350-6, *Training Special Operations Forces Infiltration/Exfiltration Operations*. 25 August 2004.

DA FORMS

DA Form 2028, Recommended Changes to Publications and Blank Forms.

DA Form 5752-R, Rope Log (Usage and History).

This page intentionally left blank.

Index

A
alternate methods of descent, 4-5
  figure-eight descender, 4-6 (illus)
  Munter hitch, 4-6 (illus)
anchor points, 1-5 (illus), 1-6 (illus), 3-6, 3-7 (illus), 3-14 (illus)
  donut ring, 3-6 (illus)
  floating safety ring, 3-7 (illus)
Australian rappel, 1-13 (illus)

B
belay safety, 1-4
belayer, 1-4
body rappel, 2-8, 2-9 (illus)
buddy-evacuation rappel, 2-14, 2-15 (illus)

C
climbing procedures, 1-13
communications, 1-18

D
deployment of ropes, 3-4
  bag technique, 3-4
  log coil technique, 3-4
donut ring, 3-6 (illus)

E
equipment, rappelling, 4-1
  inspection, 4-5
    gloves, 4-5
    helmet, 4-5
  ropes, 4-1
    dynamic, 4-2
    kermantle, 4-1 (illus)
    laid, 4-1, 4-2 (illus)
    selection, 4-2
    static, 4-2
  snaplinks, 4-3
    types, 4-3
      D-shaped, 4-4 (illus)
      locking, 4-4, 4-5 (illus)
      oval, 4-3 (illus)

F
figure-eight descender, 4-5, 4-6 (illus)
floating safety ring, 3-7 (illus)

G
ground rappelling, 2-1
  anchor point, 2-2 (illus)
  artificial anchors, 2-3
  equalized anchors, 2-3 (illus)
  establishing rappel line, 2-4
  natural anchors 2-2
  operation of rappel point, 2-5
  personnel, 2-1
    mountaineering safety officer, 2-1
    rappel lane NCO, 2-1
    rappel point commander, 2-1
  pre-equalized anchor, 2-3, 2-4 (illus)
  rappel point, 2-1, 2-2 (illus)
  recovery of rappel point, 2-7
  sustainment training, 2-1
  types of rappels, 2-7
    body rappel, 2-8, 2-9 (illus)
    buddy-evacuation rappel, 2-14 (illus), 2-15 (illus)
    hasty rappel, 2-7, 2-8 (illus)
    seat-hip rappel, 2-10 (illus)

H
hasty rappel, 2-7, 2-8 (illus)
helicopter rappelling, 3-1
  communications, 3-2
  medical coverage, 3-2
  personnel, 3-1
    belayer, 3-2
    pilot-in-command, 3-1
    rappel master, 3-1
    rappeller, 3-1
  safety briefing, 3-3
  training, 3-2
    refresher, 3-2
    sustainment, 3-2

K
knots, 5-1
  bowline, 5-14 (illus)
  bowline-on-a-bight, 5-19 (illus)
  clove hitch, 5-17 (illus)
  double fisherman's knot, 5-11 (illus)
  figure-eight bend, 5-12 (illus)
  figure-eight loop, 5-21 (illus)
  figure-eight retrace, 5-16 (illus)
  fisherman's knot, 5-10 (illus)
  frost knot, 5-26 (illus)
  girth hitch, 5-27 (illus)
  Kleimhiest knot, 5-25 (illus)
  Munter hitch, 4-6, 5-28 (illus)
  Prusik knot, 5-22 (illus)
  rappel seat, 5-29 (illus)
  round turn and two half hitches, 5-15 (illus)
  square knot, 5-9 (illus)
  transport knot, 5-24 (illus)
  tree-loop bowline, 5-23 (illus)
  two-loop figure-eight, 5-20 (illus)
  water knot, 5-13 (illus)
  wireman's knot, 5-18 (illus)

M
MH-53 helicopter
  characteristics, 3-17
  rappelling commands, 3-18
  rappelling procedures, 3-18
  rigging, 3-18
  safety, 3-19
  seating arrangements, 3-18
Munter hitch, 4-6, (illus), 5-28 (illus)

Index

N
night vision goggles, 3-3

P
personnel, ground rappelling, 2-1
  mountaineering safety officer, 2-1
  rappel lane NCO, 2-1
  rappel point commander, 2-1
personnel, helicopter rappelling, 3-1
  belayer, 3-2
  pilot-in-command, 3-1
  rappel master, 3-1
  rappeller, 3-1
pilot-in-command, 3-1
pre-equalized anchor, 2-3, 2-4 (illus)
Prusik knot, 5-22 (illus)

R
rappel anchor point, 2-2
  artificial anchors, 2-3
  natural anchors, 2-2
rappel lane, 2-4
rappel lane NCO, 1-3
rappel master, 1-1
rappel point commander, 2-1
rappel point, operation of, 2-5
  communication, 2-5 (table)
rappel point, recovery of, 2-7
rappel safety officer, 1-2
rappel seat construction, 1-7 through 1-12 (illus)
rappeller, 1-3
  preparation, 1-6
rappelling equipment, 4-1
  inspection, 4-5
    gloves, 4-5
    helmet, 4-5
  ropes, 4-1
    dynamic, 4-2
    kermantle, 4-1 (illus)
    laid, 4-1, 4-2 (illus)
    selection, 4-2
  snaplinks, 4-3
    types, 4-3
      D-shaped, 4-4 (illus)
      locking, 4-4, 4-5 (illus)
      oval, 4-3, 4-4 (illus)

rappelling procedures, 1-7
  Australian rappel, 1-13 (illus)
  climbing, 1-13
  ground, 2-1
  seat-hip rappel, 1-7, 2-10 (illus)
rope management, 5-1
  care and maintenance, 5-1
  coiling and carrying, 5-5
  inspection, 5-3
  preparation, 5-1
  rope log example, DA 5752-R, 5-2
  terminology, 5-3
  throwing, 5-8
ropes, 4-1
  dynamic, 4-2
  kermantle, 4-1 (illus)
  laid, 4-1, 4-2 (illus)
  selection, 4-2
snaplinks, 4-3
  D-shaped, 4-4 (illus)
  locking, 4-4, 4-5 (illus)
  oval, 4-3, 4-4 (illus)
static, 4-2

S
safety, 1-4
  briefing, 1-4
  tower, 1-5
seat-hip rappel, 1-7, 2-10 (illus)
snaplinks, 4-3
  D-shaped, 4-4 (illus)
  inspection, 4-5
  locking, 4-4, 4-5 (illus)
  oval, 4-3, 4-4 (illus)
static tower, 1-1 (illus)
  personnel, 1-2
    belay safety, 1-4
    belayer, 1-4
    rappel lane NCO, 1-3
      duties, 1-3
      qualifications, 1-3
      training, 1-3
    rappel master, 1-1
      duties, 1-2
      qualification, 1-2
    rappel safety officer, 1-2
    rappeller, 1-3

T
tower procedures, 1-14
  arm-and-hand signals, 1-14, 1-15 (illus)
  communications, 1-18
  UH-1H helicopter, 1-16, 1-17 (illus)
  UH-60 Blackhawk helicopter, 1-17 (illus)
  tower safety and preparation, 1-5 (illus)
  verbal commands, 1-18 (table)

U
UH-1H helicopter, 3-5 (illus)
  characteristics, 3-5
  rappelling operations 3-5
  rappelling procedures, 3-9
  rigging for rappelling, 3-5
    arm-and-hand signals, 3-10 through 3-13 (illus)
    commands, 3-10
    safety, 3-13
    seating arrangement, 3-8, 3-9 (illus)
UH-60 Blackhawk helicopter, 3-13 (illus)
  characteristics, 3-13
  rappelling operations, 3-13
  rappelling procedures, 3-16
  commands, 3-17
  rigging for rappelling, 3-13
  safety, 3-17
  seating arrangement, 3-15 (illus)

ROPE LOG (USAGE AND HISTORY)

For use of this form, see FM 3-97.61; the proponent agency is TRADOC

NSN	DOCUMENT NUMBER	SERIAL NUMBER	UNIT ID MARKING
DATE OF MFR	ISSUE DATE	DATE IN SERVICE	MFR LOT NUMBER
DIAMETER	FIBER	COLOR	LENGTH
			CONSTRUCTION

INSPECT ROPE FOR DAMAGE OR EXCESSIVE WEAR EACH TIME IT IS DEPLOYED AND AGAIN AFTER EACH USE. IMMEDIATELY RETIRE ALL SUSPECT ROPES.

DATE USED	LOCATION	TYPE OF USE	ROPE EXPOSURE	INSPECTOR'S INITIAL/DATE	ROPE CONDITION AND COMMENTS

DA FORM 5752-R, MAY 89

DATE USED	LOCATION	TYPE OF USE	ROPE EXPOSURE	INSPECTOR'S INITIAL/DATE	ROPE CONDITION AND COMMENTS

MANUAGFACTURER _____

REVERSE OF DA FORM 5752-R, MAY 89

www.ingramcontent.com/pod-product-compliance
Lightning Source LLC
Chambersburg PA
JSHW081725100526
CB00016B/2512